TOPICS AND LANGUAGE COMPETENCIES

5

MICHAEL KERWIN

SERIES ADVISOR – LEANN HOWARD

PRENTICE HALL REGENTS
A VIACOM COMPANY
Upper Saddle River, NJ 07458

Publisher: Mary Jane Peluso
Editor: Sheryl Olinsky
Development Editor: Janet Johnston
Production Supervisor: Christine Mann
Interior Design and Electronic Art: Ken Liao
Manufacturing: Ray Keating
Art Director: Merle Krumper
Cover Design: Pakhaus
Electronic Production: M.E. Aslett Corporation

PRENTICE HALL REGENTS
A VIACOM COMPANY

Printed in the United States of America

10   9   8   7   6   5   4   3

ISBN 0-13-435900-3

Prentice-Hall International (UK) Limited, London
Prentice-Hall of Australia Pty. Limited, Sydney
Prentice-Hall Canada Inc., Toronto
Prentice-Hall Hispañoamericana, S.A., Mexico
Prentice-Hall of India Private Limited, New Delhi
Prentice-Hall of Japan, Inc., Tokyo
Simon & Schuster Asia Pte. Ltd., Singapore
Editora Prentice-Hall do Brasil, Ltda., Rio de Janeiro

CONTENTS

UNIT 1: TABLES AND GRAPHS

UNIT 2: INFORMATION RESOURCES

UNIT 3: PUNCTUATING AND WRITING ENGLISH

UNIT 4: SOCIAL AGENCIES AND CONTEMPORARY SOCIETY

UNIT 5: ON THE JOB

To Peggy, Danny, Tim, Colleen and their families.

ACKNOWLEDGMENTS

This series would have never gotten off the ground without the help and encouragement of the Prentice Hall Regents specialists in California, especially Gordon Johnson, Tom Dare, and Eric Bredenberg.

To Nancy Baxer, my editor, whose encouragement, insights, and hard work brought this series to the printer.

To Leann Howard, for her valuable comments and direction.

To Sheryl Olinsky and Janet Johnston, for their sharp and patient eyes, and to Ken Liao, for his design and occasional illustrations.

To my fellow teachers and friends at the Centre de Linguistique Appliquée, Besançon, France, where it all began for me.

To all of my students throughout the world, who taught me more than they will ever know.

To Shayne West, Rad Davis, Dean Cooper, Toby Phillips, Michael Faber, and Einstein Studios for audio and music development and production.

To Karen Schultz, Meagan Mazurkewycz/Kerwin, Terry Kerwin, N. Jayne Johnston, Eric Riechman, Lizette Richards, Satish Surapaneni, Dave Dickey, Paula Williams, Louisa Hellegers, and LaTasha Artis for giving faces and voices to the characters.

To Nancy Minard and the Verona (New Jersey) Free Public Library for the library card catalog material.

To the United States Office of Consumer Affairs for information on consumer protection and complaining effectively.

To my family, who have given me the time and the space to work.

To Terry Kerwin, for her endless hours of help in the development and preparation of the text, and audio development and production.

Thank you one and all.

INTRODUCTION

Topics and Language Competencies (TLC) 5 is designed for young adult and adult ESL/ESOL students at the intermediate-high level of ESL instruction, SPL (MELT) level 5–6, CASAS ESL proficiency level B–C (208–215), and California ESL adult education level intermediate high. *TLC* covers the topics, language skills, functions, and forms established by the California English as a Second Language Model Standards for Adult Education and the CASAS ESL Competencies. *TLC* can be used alone or as a supplemental text with existing basal ESL/ESOL series to bring real-life topics, situations, skills, and materials to the classroom.

TLC 5 is designed for students who have had some exposure to English. It provides these students with topics, language functions, and language forms they need to communicate successfully. These language functions and forms are integrated with informational sources, skills, and topics that are relevant to the students' general and vocational goals. Each unit contains illustrations and realia that aid student comprehension. In addition, the <u>cassette tapes</u> provide the students with realistic language as it is used outside the classroom. <u>Teacher's guides</u> are available to provide both less experienced and master teachers with a variety of ideas on how to use the material meaningfully in the classroom.

In each unit, *TLC* integrates all of the four language skills — listening/speaking, grammar, reading, and writing. Picture pages give the students a visual representation of vocabulary, people, places, and objects they will encounter throughout the book. <u>Scenes</u> feature realistic conversations that the students hear on the cassette, followed by selective listening tasks and practices. <u>Practices</u> give the students a chance to work with realia, such as forms and applications, similar to those they will encounter outside the classroom. Pair and group work activities give the students the opportunity to have fun with language and use it creatively. <u>Lifeskills/Workskills</u> present the students with content relevant to their personal and vocational goals. <u>Cross-Cultural Discussions</u> allow the students to discuss aspects of their own cultures, such as educational systems, and to compare and contrast them to aspects of U.S. culture. <u>Supplemental Activities</u> provide additional opportunities for students to learn about, ask for, and receive social and factual information. In the <u>Summary</u>, the students check off the functions, forms, and topics learned in the unit.

TO THE TEACHER

Icons are used throughout *TLC* to indicate to you and your students what type of activity follows. Here are suggestions on how to use the material.

 Play the tape. After the first listening, ask the students questions so they know what to listen for as you play the tape the second time. Possible questions are "Where is the scene taking place?" "Who are the characters?" "What are the characters doing?" Go over the directions for the listening task. Play the tape again and have the students complete the listening task. Correct and evaluate their work individually, or go over it with the whole class.

 Either have the students cover the dialogue in their books and listen to the conversation on the tape, or have them follow along with the book while they are listening to the tape.

 Tasks with this icon check students' comprehension and ability to express themselves in writing. You may want to model or demonstrate individual exercises on the board. Have the students complete the task in their books. Then correct and evaluate their work individually, or go over the task with the whole class.

 Tasks with this icon have students interact with each other in English to practice various language skills and tasks in different situations. Start by modeling each exercise for the class. Assign each student a partner and give the partners a time frame to complete the exercise. Be sure to give each pair enough time to complete the task and then change roles. Walk around the classroom to observe, encourage, and provide assistance to each of the pairs. When all the pairs have finished, ask a few of them to perform their work for the rest of the class.

 Activities with this icon are group discussion tasks. Explain and describe the task or topic and the procedures for participating. Set a time frame. Then ask for a volunteer from each group to be the discussion leader for the group. If no one volunteers, appoint a discussion leader. Encourage all students to participate in their groups. If necessary, get involved with groups yourself to promote more conversation. Ask for a volunteer student to summarize the group's findings and to present the findings to the class.

Information with this icon is optional and is included as a reference for students and teachers. Although the information may be somewhat difficult for some students, others may find it a stimulating challenge.

Unit 1 Tables and Graphs

TOPICS

▲ Statistical information
▲ Tables
▲ Charts
▲ Bar graphs, line graphs, and circle graphs
▲ Range, median, and average (mean)

LANGUAGE FUNCTIONS

On completion, students will have used English for:

▲ factual information: to illustrate, to conclude, to infer.
▲ social and interpersonal relations: to approve or disapprove.
▲ suasion: to predict consequences.

LANGUAGE FORMS

On completion, students will have used the following structures:

▲ **Sentence types**

Conjunctive adverbs: "therefore," "however"

Adverbial clauses of concession: "unless," "although"

▲ **Verb tenses**

Modals related to past events: "should have," "could have," "would have," "might have," "must have"

LANGUAGE SKILLS

Listening: On completion, students will have:

▲ demonstrated understanding of most face-to-face speech in standard dialect and at a normal spoken rate, with some repetition.
▲ demonstrated understanding of abstract topics in familiar contexts.
▲ demonstrated understanding of new vocabulary in context through guessing strategies.

Speaking: On completion, students will have:

▲ asked and answered questions fluently with minimal errors in the present, past, and future tenses.
▲ clarified meaning through strategies such as paraphrasing when misunderstanding occurs.
▲ adjusted the level of language used in face-to-face conversations in accordance with the formality required by the social situation.

Reading: On completion, students will have:

▲ interpreted both authentic and edited materials.
▲ identified main ideas and supporting details or examples from familiar material.
▲ made inferences.

Writing: On completion, students will have:

▲ expanded and combined simple sentences by adding modifying words, clauses, and phrases.
▲ written and punctuated complex sentences.
▲ taken simple notes from public announcements, short lectures, and real interviews.

Tables and Graphs

Topics: Conveying information in graphic form, recognizing types of graphics

Look at the table, the graphs, and the chart. Write the correct description for each and the type of information it contains. Then check your work with a partner. Take turns describing the information contained in each group.

Partner's name _____

Use these words.

line graph	table	daily production	bar graph
pie chart	the weather	a budget	monthly sales

Figure I

ACME COMPUTER SALES: DOLLAR TOTALS JANUARY THROUGH JUNE

Month	Sales
January	$1,025,525.00
February	1,624,987.00
March	2,511,853.00
April	2,069,000.00
May	3,000,285.00
June	3,585,000.00
	$18,816,650.00

Type __Table_____

Information _____

Figure II

ACME COMPUTER SALES: UNIT SALES WEEK OF 5/12

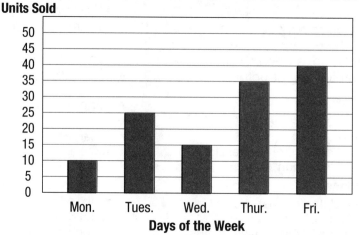

Type of graph _____

Information _____

Tables and Graphs

Topics: Conveying information in graphic form, recognizing types of graphics

Figure III

HIGH AND LOW TEMPERATURES FOR ONE WEEK

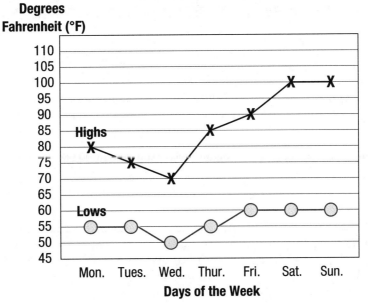

Type of graph _____

Information _____

Figure IV

MARIO DIEGO'S MONTHLY BUDGET

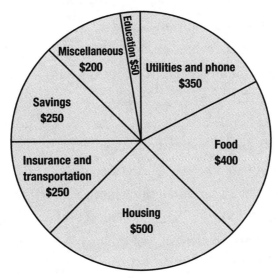

Type of graph _____

Information _____

Acme Computer Sales Grow!

Topic: Reading a table

ACME COMPUTER SALES: DOLLAR TOTALS JANUARY THROUGH JUNE

Month	Sales
January	$1,025,525.00
February	1,624,987.00
March	2,511,853.00
April	2,069,000.00
May	3,000,285.00
June	3,585,000.00
	$18,816,650.00

Listen.

> Good morning, ladies and gentlemen. As you can see from the table, Acme Computer sales continue to grow by leaps and bounds! In the first six months of this year, we've gone from sales of just over a million dollars in January to over three and a half million this month alone. Total sales for these six months are close to nineteen million dollars. That's 50 percent more than last year for the same time period. Keep up the good work!

Listen again and look at the table. Answer the questions, using the information contained in the talk and in the table. Then check your answers with a partner.

Partner's name _____

1. What were the total sales in January? $_____

2. Were sales higher in January or in June? _____

3. Was the sales manager happy about the sales report? Why?

    _____

    _____

4. What do you think "leaps and bounds" means?

    _____ Slow but steady   _____ Quick   _____ Other: _____

5. What were Acme Computer sales last year for the same time period?

    _____ $18,000,000   _____ $27,000,000   _____ $12,400,000

6. Do you ever have to read or use tables in your work, at home, or at school? When? What kind of tables?

    _____

    _____

    _____

Reading a Table, Graph, or Chart

Topic: Interpreting a table, graph, or chart

Tips on How to Read a Table, Graph, or Chart

1. First, look at the table, graph, or chart for an overall impression. Ask yourself: What kind of graphic is it? What does it represent?

2. Read the title. This will contain the what, where, and when of the information.

3. Determine the scale or unit of measure in the graphic, such as dollars, units sold, days, months, or years.

4. Check the headings, both vertical and horizontal. These tell you what is being represented and the values.

Use the table, graphs, and chart on pages 2 and 3 to answer the questions. Then check your answers with a partner.

Partner's name _____

1. Type of table, graph, or chart:

   Figure I   _____   Figure III _____

   Figure II   _____   Figure IV _____

2. Title:

   Figure I   _____

   Figure II   _____

   Figure III _____

   Figure IV   _____

3. Unit of measure:

   Figure II   _____

   Figure III _____

   Figure IV   _____

4. Headings:

   Figure I   _____   _____

   Figure II   vertical _____

               horizontal _____

   Figure III vertical _____

               horizontal _____

   Figure IV   _____   _____

               _____   _____

               _____   _____

               _____

Let's Look at a Bar Graph.

Scene 2

Topic: Elements of a bar graph

> Statistic = a number that represents numerical data
> (ex.: temperatures, sales, number of people)
> Graphs and charts = pictorial displays showing comparisons and trends
> Types of graphs: bar graphs, line graphs, pie charts (circle graphs)

Listen.

Good morning, class. Today we are going to take a look at different types of statistical representation. As you know, a statistic is a number that represents data or information. Statistics are used every day in business reports, on television, in newspapers and magazines, in textbooks, and in other sources of information. A statistic can be anything from the temperature on a given day, to the sales for the day, month, or year, to the number of students in a class.

Graphs and charts present statistics in an easily understandable fashion. Graphs and charts show comparisons and trends. We are going to look at the most common graphs and charts: bar graphs, line graphs, and circle graphs, usually called pie charts.

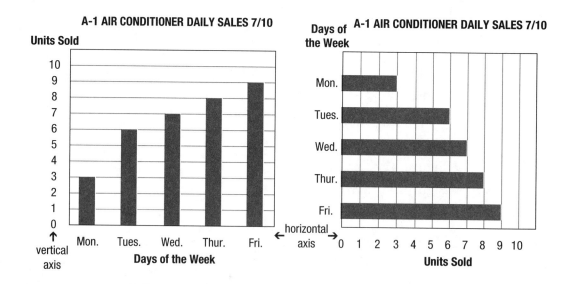

First, let's look at a bar graph. A bar graph shows or compares statistics or information. As you can see, a bar graph can be displayed horizontally or vertically—that is, the same information can be shown in two different layouts by switching the two axes. The length (or height) of each bar represents a specific value. The horizontal axis usually represents time, and the vertical axis usually represents a quantity or value, as in the graph on the left.

Let's Look at a Bar Graph. (continued)

Topic: Elements of a bar graph

> In the example on the left, the vertical heading is **Units Sold**, and the horizontal heading is **Days of the Week**. (In the example on the right, these are reversed.) Both graphs show the number of units sold for each day of the week. When you look at the bar above Tuesday in the left-hand graph and follow it across to the vertical axis on the left, it is easy to see that on Tuesday, six units were sold. Also, with a quick glance you can see that more units were sold on Friday than on Monday.
>
> Of course, this or any information is not worth anything by itself; it's what you do with it that's important.

Listen again. Use the space below to take notes on the lecture.

_____

_____

_____

_____

_____

_____

Listen to the lecture again. Then use your notes to answer the questions.

1. What is a statistic?

   _____

   _____

2. Write two ways graphs and charts can be used.

   _____

   _____

3. What do the bar graphs on the board (see pg. 6) represent?

   _____

   _____

4. Do you ever use statistics, graphs, or charts? Explain.

   _____

   _____

Reading and Making Bar Graphs

Topic: Understanding a bar graph

KOOL AIR CONDITIONING DAILY SALES 7/10

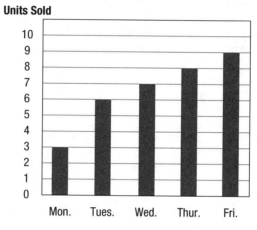

Units Sold

Days of the Week

Use the information on the bar graph to answer the questions in complete sentences. Then check your answers with a partner.

Partner's name _____

1. On which day were the fewest units sold? How many were sold that day?

   _____

   _____

2. How many units were sold on Thursday?

   _____

3. Did sales increase or decrease from Monday to Friday?

   _____

4. On which days were more than six units sold?

   _____

   _____

5. If you were the manager of the store and wanted to close one day a week, which day would you close? Why?

   _____

   _____

Reading and Making Bar Graphs
(continued)

Topic: Rendering statistics as a bar graph

Monthly production at Allied Bikes:			
Month	Units Produced (in hundreds)	Month	Units Produced (in hundreds)
January	30	April	33
February	28	May	28
March	31	June	30

Use the monthly production information for Allied Bikes to complete the bar graph. Add a title. Then compare your graph with a partner's.

Partner's name _____

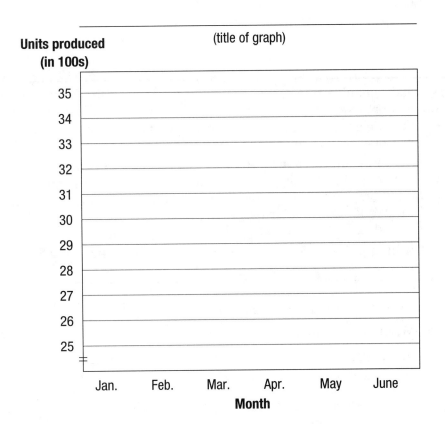

Work with a partner. Ask and answer questions about your graphs.

Partner's name _____

A Line Graph Shows Trends.

Scene 3

Topic: Reading and understanding a line graph

DAILY HIGHS AND LOWS FOR THE WEEK OF 8/1

Temperature (°F)

Highs

Lows

Days of the Week

Mon.   Tues.   Wed.   Thur.   Fri.   Sat.   Sun.

OK, everyone, please take a seat and we'll begin. In the first part of the lecture, we talked about statistics and bar graphs. Now let's take a look at another type of graph: the line graph. A line graph shows trends—that is, whether a value is increasing, decreasing, fluctuating, or staying the same.

In the example on the board, the high and low temperatures for a week are shown. When we look at the top line, which represents the highs, we can readily see that the temperature decreased from Monday to Tuesday and again from Tuesday to Wednesday. It's also easy to see a warming trend from Wednesday through Sunday.

Now, while I put up this other graph, I want you to open your books to page 5 and look over "Tips on How to Read a Table, Graph, or Chart."

 Look at the graph and answer the questions.

1. What was the highest temperature for the week?

   Temperature _____   Day of the week _____

2. What was the lowest temperature for the week?

   Temperature _____   Day of the week _____

3. What do you think the high and low will be on Monday? Why?

   High _____   Low _____

   Reason: _____

Making a Line Graph

Topic: Rendering statistics as a line graph

Use the monthly sales information for Acme Computer to complete the line graph. Add the title. Then compare your graph with a partner's.

Partner's name _____

	Sales ($ in millions)		Sales ($ in millions)
January	1.0	July	4.0
February	1.5	August	3.5
March	2.5	September	3.5
April	2.0	October	2.5
May	3.0	November	2.0
June	3.5	December	1.5

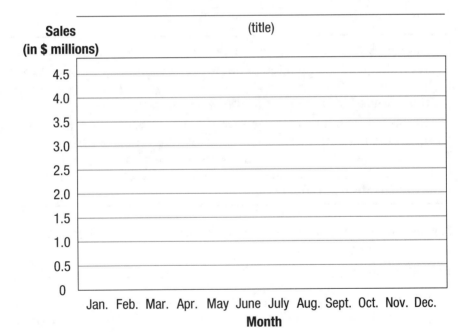

Use complete sentences to describe the line graph in your own words. Use some of these words.

highest	lowest	value	represent	vertical
horizontal	trend	increase	decrease	

_____

_____

_____

Name _____   **Date** _____

Scene
4

Let's Look at a Circle Graph/Pie Chart.

Topic: Understanding a circle graph/pie chart

MARIO DIEGO'S MONTHLY BUDGET

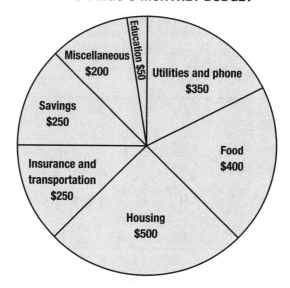

Listen.

Let's look at a circle graph on the board as we continue with the lecture.

A circle graph or pie chart shows the relationship of a part to the whole. The whole circle represents the whole quantity. Each section or slice of the circle stands for some part of the whole quantity.

In the example on the board we see Mario's budget. The entire circle represents his entire budget, with each slice representing a part of the whole. Looking at the graph, we can see that housing and food make up almost half of Mario's total budget, and education makes up the smallest part of the entire budget.

Listen again. Answer the questions in complete sentences. Then check your answers with a partner.

Partner's name _____

1. What takes up the largest single part of Mario's budget?

   _____

   _____

   _____

2. What takes up the smallest single part of Mario's budget?

   _____

   _____

   _____

3. Does Mario budget more for utilities or for savings?

   _____

   _____

4. Mario wants to buy a new car, but he needs to save an additional fifty dollars a month to do so. What can Mario do to save more?

   _____

   _____

   _____

   _____

Name _____   Date _____

Drawing a Circle Graph/Pie Chart

Topic: Constructing a circle graph

 Use Acme Computer's budget information to complete the circle graph. (HINT: Before you begin, find the total *monthly budget.) Then compare your graph with a partner's.*

Partner's name _____

ACME COMPUTER MONTHLY BUDGET	
Rent	$50,000
Supplies	$30,000
Salary	$40,000
Advertising	$70,000
Miscellaneous	$10,000

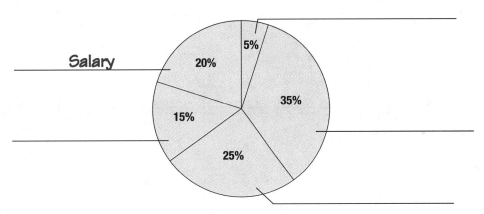

Salary — 20%

5%

35%

15%

25%

Total monthly budget: _____

 Describe the circle graph in your own words, using complete sentences. Use some of these words.

divided	portion	part	percent of	largest
smallest	compared to	distribution	slice	

_____

_____

_____

_____

_____

_____

A Flowchart Shows the Steps in a Problem.

Topics: Flowcharts, symbols

A flowchart graphically shows the steps in the solution of a problem or the sequence of operations in or for a program or task. In flowcharts, symbols and words support one another. When we write a brief description within the symbols, it makes a logical progression, sequence of operations, or chain of command easier to understand than words or symbols alone.

Here is a system flowchart.

| Input $\longrightarrow$ Process $\longrightarrow$ Output |

First the information or data is entered into the system. Then it is processed, and finally the processed information is given out.

Now look at a program flowchart.

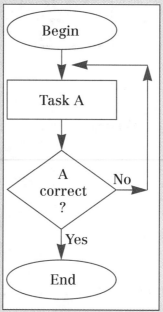

After beginning the program, the computer performs Task A. After completing the task, the computer checks the data to see if the task has been completed correctly. If Task A has not been completed correctly, the computer is instructed to go back to the beginning and begin again. If the task has been completed correctly, the computer continues to the end of the program.

The symbols used in flowcharts are standardized and have special meaning.

The flow or order is represented by arrows.

A circle or oval is used to represent a starting point, ending point, or a "go to" another point in the system.

A rectangle is used to show a specific purpose.

A diamond is used to represent a choice or branching opportunity.

Understanding and Making a Flowchart

Topic: Components of a flowchart

 Read Scene 5 again. Then match the words and symbols on the left with the correct term or definition on the right. Check your answers with a partner.

Partner's name _____

1. ◯ *or* ⬭ ___d___   a. Represented by arrows.

2. flowchart ___   b. Represents a choice or branching opportunity.

3. ▭ ___   c. A graphic representation of a solution to a problem or order of operation.

4. flow ___   d. Represents a starting point, ending point, or "go to" another point.

5. ◇ ___   e. Represents a specific purpose.

 Work with a partner. Fill in the flowchart with the correct phrases for each step.

Partner's name _____

Use these words.

check product quality
produce new product
package for shipping
pass/fail inspection

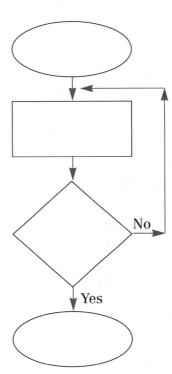

Lifeskills/
Workskills

1

Figuring Range, Median, and Average (Mean)

Course	Number of students	Course	Number of students
Computer 1	16	ESL 4	13
Computer 2	13	GED	18
ESL 1	17	Math 1	12
ESL 2	20	Math 2	11
ESL 3	15		

To find the range, the median, and the average (mean) of a group of numbers, first put the numbers in descending order of value, from the highest/largest to the lowest/smallest.

Course	Number of students
ESL 2	20
GED	18
ESL 1	17
Computer 1	16
ESL 3	15 ◄─── **Median**
Computer 2	13
ESL 4	13
Math 1	12
Math 2	11

The **range** is the highest/largest value minus the lowest/smallest value. The range for the example is from 20 students (in ESL 2) to 11 students (in Math 2), a range of 9 (20 minus 11).

The **median** is the middle value—that is, the value that falls in the exact middle of the series. In a list with an odd number of items, the median has the same number of values above it and below it. In the example, 15 is the median: four values are higher, and four are lower. In a series with an even number of values, the median is the number exactly between the *two middle* numbers.

 Figure the range and the median for each series of numbers.

Temperature	Distance
45 degrees	92 miles
40 degrees	80 miles
37 degrees	63 miles
22 degrees	60 miles
20 degrees	60 miles
18 degrees	56 miles
17 degrees	54 miles

Median: _____ degrees   Median: _____ miles

Range: _____ degrees   Range: _____ miles

Lifeskills/ Workskills

1

Figuring Range, Median, and Average (Mean) (continued)

The **average (mean)** of a set of values is found by two steps.

Step 1: Add all the values.
Step 2: Divide the total by the number of items. The answer is the average.

Look at the first example on page 16. Find the average number of students in the courses.

Total number of students: $\dfrac{135}{9}$
Divide by total number of classes

Average number in the courses: 15

Answer the questions about the table and graphs on pages 2 and 3. Check your answers with a partner.

Partner's name _____

1. Find the range for

   Figure I.   Range: _____   From _____ to _____

   Figure II.   Range: _____   From _____ to _____

   Figure III.   Range: _____   From _____ to _____

2. Find the median for

   Figure II.   _____   (High _____   Low _____)

   Figure III.   _____   (High _____   Low _____)

3. Find the average for

   Figure II.   _____

   Figure III.   _____

Collecting and Presenting Statistical Information

Topics: Statistics, tables, graphs, charts, resources, and graphic presentation

Task 1:

Bring to class an example of each type of statistical information: a table, a bar graph, a line graph, and a pie chart. Visit your town or school library and look in encyclopedias, in newspapers, in almanacs, or in any other sources of information.

Task 2:

Work with a partner. Pick one of the topics below to research. Then decide which type of graph would be the best way to present the information you collect. Make the graph and describe it and its content to a group or to the entire class.

Partner's name _____

Topics:

- The local temperatures for the week.
- Your favorite sports team's win/loss record.
- Your monthly budget.
- Class attendance.
- Population of your home country or where you live now.
- How you spend your time Monday–Friday.
- Other: _____
  _____

Your topic: _____

Your graph: Include title, units of measurement, and headings. When presenting your graph to the class, identify or note any trends or comparisons.

Name _____   Date _____

Summary: Tables and Graphs Checklist

Check (✓) one.

Yes	No	Need more practice	
☐	☐	☐	I can read and interpret a simple table. (example: p. 4. *"Sales were higher in June."*)
☐	☐	☐	I can read, interpret, and draw a bar graph. (example: p. 8. *"Eight units were sold on Thursday."*)
☐	☐	☐	I can read, interpret, and draw a line graph. (example: p. 11. *"The highest sales for the year were in July."*)
☐	☐	☐	I can read, interpret, and draw a circle graph/pie chart. (example: p. 12. *"Mario budgets more for savings."*)
☐	☐	☐	I can determine the range, median, and average of a group of numbers. (example: p. 16. *"The range for the example is 9."*)
☐	☐	☐	I can collect and present statistical information. (example: p. 18)

Write two other things you can say or do in English.

I can _____ .

I can _____ .

_____
Signature

Teacher's comments: _____

_____

Unit 2 Information Resources

TOPICS

- ▲ Information sources
- ▲ Library card catalogs
- ▲ Almanacs
- ▲ Computer software
- ▲ Newspapers
- ▲ Educational systems

LANGUAGE FUNCTIONS

On completion, students will have used English for:

- ▲ factual information: to illustrate, to conclude, to infer.

LANGUAGE FORMS

On completion, students will have used the following structures:

- ▲ **Sentence types**

  Conjunctive adverbs: "therefore," "however"

  Adverbial clauses of concession: "unless," "although"

LANGUAGE SKILLS

Listening: On completion, students will have:

- ▲ demonstrated understanding of the majority of face-to-face speech in standard dialect and at a normal spoken rate, with some repetition.
- ▲ demonstrated understanding of abstract topics in familiar contexts.
- ▲ demonstrated understanding of new vocabulary in context through guessing strategies.

Speaking: On completion, students will have:

- ▲ asked and answered questions fluently with minimal errors in the present, past, and future tenses.
- ▲ participated with increasing fluency in most face-to-face social conversations.
- ▲ clarified meaning through strategies such as paraphrasing when misunderstanding occurs.

Reading: On completion, students will have:

- ▲ interpreted both authentic and edited materials.
- ▲ identified main ideas and supporting details or examples from familiar material.
- ▲ guessed meaning from context by analyzing words.
- ▲ made inferences.
- ▲ summarized reading passages.

Writing: On completion, students will have:

- ▲ expanded and combined simple sentences by adding modifying words, clauses, and phrases.
- ▲ written and punctuated complex sentences.

Sources of Information

Topics: Print and technological resources

  Look at the different sources of information. Write one or two kinds of information you could find in each source. Compare your answers with a partner's.

Partner's name _____

_____
_____

_____
_____

_____
_____

_____
_____

_____
_____

_____
_____

_____
_____

_____
_____

The Library

Topic: A library's departments and components

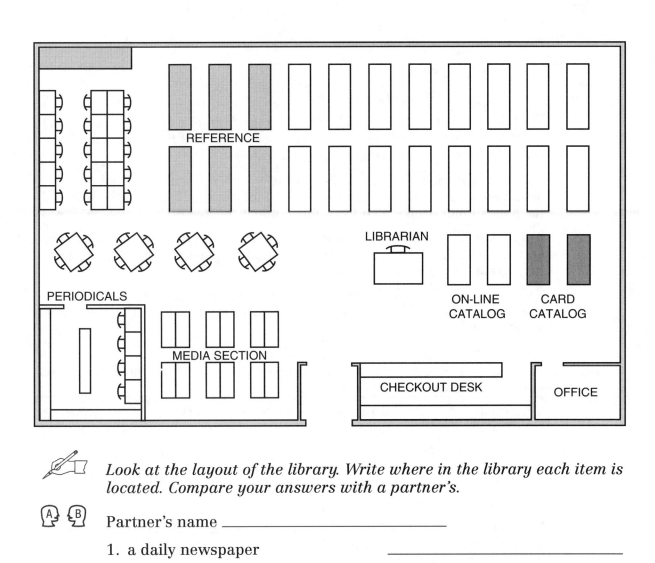

Look at the layout of the library. Write where in the library each item is located. Compare your answers with a partner's.

Partner's name _____

1. a daily newspaper _____
2. an encyclopedia _____
3. an audiotape or videotape _____
4. information about the Civil War _____
5. a book by John Steinbeck _____
6. The current issue of *Time* Magazine _____

Where Would You Look?

Topic: Sources of information

 Read the descriptions of resources.

Table of contents   A list usually found in the front of a book or magazine. It lists the subjects or topics in the text (the contents) and their page numbers, in the order they appear in the text.

Index   A list usually found in the back of a book or catalog. It contains, in alphabetical order, the names, places, and information found in the text and the page numbers on which the information is located.

Almanac   An annual publication that includes a calendar, weather forecasts, astronomical information, tide tables, and other statistical information related to the year and its seasonal changes.

Encyclopedia   A set of columns that include articles on places, persons, things, and ideas, in alphabetical order. Entries are arranged like entries in a dictionary or index.

Dictionary   A book that lists, in alphabetical order, words and their meanings. Each listing includes the word's pronunciation, origin/derivation, development, and part of speech.

Thesaurus   A book of words and concepts. A thesaurus also lists synonyms (words with similar meanings) and antonyms (words with opposite meanings).

Atlas   A book of maps and charts. Relief maps show mountains, valleys, rivers, and other physical characteristics of each country or region. Political maps show national, state, county, and city boundaries. Road maps show transportation connections.

Newspapers and periodicals   A section of the library that contains local and national newspapers, plus magazines (periodicals) published at regular intervals, such as weekly or monthly.

Reader's Guide to Periodical Literature   A publication that lists published magazines by name, issue number, date, title, and author.

Library card catalog   A file of drawers of cards in alphabetical order. Each book, periodical, and periodical article in the library can be looked up in the card catalog by title, by author, and by subject.

Computer information systems/on-line catalog   A software program that contains the same information as a card catalog, plus the books and periodicals in nearby libraries with which the library's computer is connected. The information is obtained from computers which the librarians train the public to use. When a library receives a new book or periodical, the book or periodical is added to the library's card catalog and on-line catalog.

Locating Information in the Library

Topic: Information sources

Refer to Scene 6 and write where you would look for the information. Check your answers with a partner.

Partner's name _____

1. the population of France _____
2. the capital of Brazil _____
3. the meaning of "capitalize" _____
   _____
4. information on Abraham Lincoln _____
   _____
5. today's news _____
6. tomorrow's weather forecast _____
7. the shortest route from Los Angeles to Dallas _____
   _____
8. who discovered electricity _____
9. last year's weather _____
10. the author of *War and Peace* _____

Make up questions to ask your partner.

Partner's name _____

Examples:
  What's the longest river in the United States?
  What are the name and the height of the world's tallest mountain?
  Name three books written by Charles Dickens.

_____

_____

_____

_____

_____

_____

The Card Catalog Helps You Locate Books.

Scene 7

Topic: Library card catalogs

The card catalog helps you locate books in the library. It is a series of drawers arranged alphabetically that contain the cards. A library card catalog is usually divided into two sections: Title/Author drawers and Subject drawers.

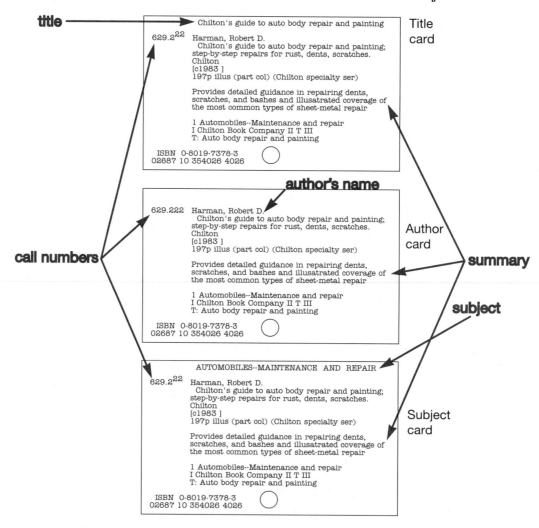

Each card lists the title, author, and call number of a book. The call number is found in the upper-left corner of the card. The call number tells where the book can be found in the library: in the section containing Fiction, Biography, Mystery, etc.

To find a book in the card catalog:

1. • Look up the title of the book. *or*
   • Look up the author's last name. *or*
   • Look up the subject of the book to find its title.

2. • Write down the call number and use it to locate the book you're looking for on the shelf.

Using a Card Catalog

Topic: Library card catalogs

Read the cards and answer the questions.

```
641.8     Beranbaum, Rose Levy
            The cake bible. Ed by Maria D. Guarnaschelli.
          Morrow [c1988]
          556p illus (part col)

          Providing countless solutions and tips for commonly
          encountered baking problems, this comprehensive
          cake cookbook provides precise instructions for
          baking and decorating spectacular special-occasion
          cakes of any size up to eighteen inches in diameter

          1 Cake     I Ed     II T


   ISBN  0-688-04402-6
   12026    62705    851712                        8324
```

1. Type of card _____
   Call number _____
   Title _____

```
             The cake bible
641.8     Beranbaum, Rose Levy
B           The cake bible. Ed by Maria D. Guarnaschelli.
          Morrow [c1988]
          556p illus (part col)

          Providing countless solutions and tips for commonly
          encountered baking problems, this comprehensive
          cake cookbook provides precise instructions for
          baking and decorating spectacular special-occasion
          cakes of any size up to eighteen inches in diameter

          1 Cake     I Ed     II T


   ISBN  0-688-04402-6
   12026    62705    851712                        8324
```

2. Type of card _____
   Name of Editor _____
   ISBN _____

```
            COMEDIANS--BIOGRAPHY
B         Benny, Jack
BENNY       Sunday nights at seven; the Jack Benny story, by
          Jack Benny and his daughter, Joan.
          Warner Bks [c1990 ]
          300p

          The unfinished memoir of the late comedian is
          interwoven with reminiscences by his daughter in
          an anecdotal biography of the golden age of
          television and of the celebrities of the era

          1 Comedians--Biography     I Jt auth
          II T

   ISBN  0-466-51546-9
   07554    36650    314051                        0304
```

3. Type of card _____
   Title _____
   Category _____

```
B         Benny, Jack
BENNY       Sunday nights at seven; the Jack Benny story, by
          Jack Benny and his daughter, Joan.
          Warner Bks [c1990 ]
          300p

          The unfinished memoir of the late comedian is
          interwoven with reminiscences by his daughter in
          an anecdotal biography of the golden age of
          television and of the celebrities of the era

          1 Comedians--Biography     I Jt auth
          II T

   ISBN  0-466-51546-9                       90-50286
   07554    36650    314051                        0304
```

4. Type of card _____
   Co-author _____
   Is there a call number? _____
   What appears in its place?

   _____

Choose a Search Option by Number.

Topic: Using the computer search to find a book

Many card catalogs are now listed on computer. This allows titles, authors, and subjects to be found with a few simple commands. It also shows the availability of a book.

Look at the computer screens and listen.

```
                   Library Search
Choose a search option by number.
            1: Author
            2: Title
            3: Subject
            4: Quit searching
Enter a number: ___ and press "Enter"
Commands:   SO = Start Over   B = Back   ? = HELP
```

Screen 1: Choose the type of search you want. For example, if you know the author's name, type in "1" for author and press "Enter."

```
                   Author Search
Author: last name, first name
            Example: Asimov, Isaac
Enter author (last name, first): _____
and press "Enter"
Commands:   SO = Start Over   B = Back   ? = HELP
```

Screen 2: Type in the author's last name and then first name; press "Enter." For example, if the author's last name is Steinbeck, type that in and press "Enter."

```
              Your Search: Steinbeck
       Author                Titles
1. Steinbeck, Allan            4
2. Steinbeck Conference        1
3. Steinbeck, John            23
Enter a line number for more detail: ___ and press
"Enter"
Commands:   SO = Start Over   B = Back   ? = HELP
```

Screen 3: Enter the line number of the author you want. For example, if you want a book by John Steinbeck, enter "3."

```
           Your Search: Steinbeck, John
       Author                Date
1. Steinbeck, John
     Burning Bright: A Play    1967
2. Steinbeck, John
     Cannery Row               1945
3. Steinbeck, John
     Of Mice and Men           1937
Enter a line number for more detail or press "A" for
more titles: ___ and press "Enter"
Commands:   SO = Start Over   B = Back   ? = HELP
```

Screen 4: Type in the line number for the title you're looking for and press "Enter." For example, if the book you're looking for is *Cannery Row*, type in "2" and press "Enter."

```
Author: Steinbeck, John
Title: Cannery Row
Publisher: Viking Press, 1945
Call Number: F581940
Number of Copies: 6
Status: Available
Commands:   SO = Start Over   B = Back
            Return = Next Screen
```

Screen 5: This is the listing for *Cannery Row* by John Steinbeck.

Listen again. Follow the directions to complete the entry on each screen.

Practice 8

Using the Computer Search

Topic: A library computer search

Look at the computer screens on the opposite page and answer the questions. Then check your answers with a partner.

Partner's name _____

1. What would you enter on the first screen if you want a book about American sports? _____

2. What would you enter in the first box if you want a book entitled *Great Expectations*? _____

3. What would you enter on the first screen if you don't understand the directions and want some help? _____

4. What would you enter on the second screen if the book you want is written by Pearl Buck?

   _____

5. What would you enter on the second screen if the book you want is written by someone with the last name of Piper?

   _____

6. What would you enter on the second screen if you want a book by Allan Steinbeck? _____

7. What would you enter on the third screen if you want to begin the search again? _____

8. What would you enter on the fourth screen if you want a play by John Steinbeck? _____

9. What would you enter on the fourth screen if you can't remember the title of the book you want but do remember that it was published before *Cannery Row*? _____

10. What would you enter on the fifth screen if you want to go back to the previous screen? _____

11. Look at screen 5. Who published *Cannery Row*? _____ When was it published? _____

A Software Program Instructs the Computer.

Scene 9

Topic: Software packages

A software program instructs the computer to perform specific instructions in a specific order. It instructs the computer what to do and when. Software programs are written by computer programmers and are stored on tape, on a floppy disk, on the computer's hard drive, or on a CD-ROM. There are basically two kinds of software: system software and application software.

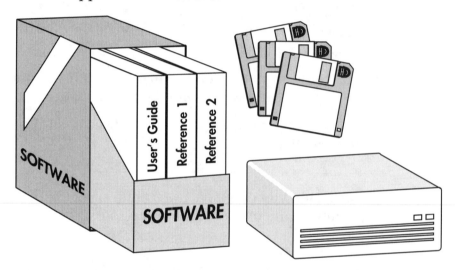

Application software is specific software for particular user applications. A computer game, a word-processing program, a payroll or accounts receivable program, and computer-assisted instruction programs (CAI) are all examples of application software. Application software programs make up the majority of software programs on the market today.

System software allows the user to run/use the different types of application software mentioned above. The disk operating system (DOS) is an example of system software. The disk operating system permits the user to instruct or program the computer to run different application systems. System software is usually supplied by the manufacturer of the computer and may be a component of the computer when it is purchased.

Application Software	System Software
Games	Operating system (DOS)
Word processing	Programming languages
Computer-assisted instruction (CAI)	Utility programs
Encyclopedia or dictionary	

Understanding Software-Specific Language

Topic: Computer software terminology

Read Scene 9 again and use complete sentences to answer the questions. Check your answers with a partner.

Ⓐ Ⓑ Partner's name _____

1. In line 2, what does "it" refer to?

   _____

   _____

2. What tells the computer what to do and when to do it?

   _____

   _____

3. How is software stored?

   _____

   _____

4. What does "CAI" stand for?

   _____

   _____

5. What is application software?

   _____

   _____

6. What is system software?

   _____

   _____

7. How do system and application software work together?

   _____

   _____

   _____

Lifeskills/ Workskills

Summarizing a Newspaper Article

In a local or other daily newspaper, find an article about each of the subjects. Read each article and write a short summary.

1. A recent local or national event _____
(source)

   Title of article _____

   Summary: _____

   _____

   _____

2. A recent sporting event _____
(source)

   Title of article _____

   Summary: _____

   _____

   _____

3. A local or national social problem _____
(source)

   Title of article _____

   Summary: _____

   _____

   _____

4. Local or national business news _____
(source)

   Title of article _____

   Summary: _____

   _____

   _____

5. Arts or entertainment _____
(source)

   Title of article _____

   Summary: _____

   _____

   _____

Educational Systems

Read the statements and questions and write a few thoughts on each point. Are your thoughts on each topic the same now as they were when you came to this country? Discuss your thoughts with a small group. One person takes notes and reports your discussion to the class.

1. Education should be neither free nor compulsory.

   _____

   _____

   _____

   _____

2. What are the advantages and/or disadvantages of bilingual classes?

   _____

   _____

   _____

   _____

3. Should religion be taught in public schools? Why or why not? Should a particular religion be taught? Which?

   _____

   _____

   _____

   _____

4. Should all children be tested for intelligence and placed into educational, technical, or trade classes and programs according to their scores? Why or why not?

   _____

   _____

   _____

   _____

Information Researching Tasks

Choose one of the tasks to do for class.

Task 1:

Visit your school or town library to find the call numbers for the titles, authors, or subjects used in Practice 6 (page 25). Answer the questions. Check your answers with a partner.

Partner's name _____

Listing	Call number	Listing	Call number
1. _____	_____	6. _____	_____
2. _____	_____	7. _____	_____
3. _____	_____	8. _____	_____
4. _____	_____	9. _____	_____
5. _____	_____	10. _____	_____

Task 2:

Visit a computer software store and find one example for each of the types of software listed. Write the name of the program and its price.

	Title	Price
1. a word-processing program	_____	_____
2. an encyclopedia on a CD-ROM	_____	_____
3. a game	_____	_____
4. an educational program	_____	_____
5. a business program	_____	_____

Summary: Resources Checklist

Check (✓) one.

Yes	No	Need more practice	
☐	☐	☐	I can talk about various sources of information. (example: p. 24. *"An atlas is a book of maps and charts."*)
☐	☐	☐	I can understand and use a card catalog. (example: p. 26. *"The card catalog is divided into Title/Author and Subject drawers."*)
☐	☐	☐	I can use the library computer search. (example: p. 28. *"Type in the author's last name and then first name."*)
☐	☐	☐	I can read and talk about different types of software. (example: p. 30. *"There are two kinds of software: system and application."*)
☐	☐	☐	I can find and read various kinds of articles in the newspaper. (example: p. 32.)
☐	☐	☐	I can use a library card catalog to find various titles, authors, and subjects. (example: p. 34.)

Write two other things you can say or do in English.

I can _____ .
I can _____ .

_____
Signature

Teacher's comments: _____
_____

Unit ③ Punctuating and Writing English

TOPICS

▲ Punctuation
▲ Paragraph organization
▲ Paragraph writing
▲ Letter writing
▲ Business letters

LANGUAGE FUNCTIONS

On completion, students will have used English for:

▲ factual information: to illustrate, to conclude, to infer.
▲ social and interpersonal relations: to approve, to disapprove, to express indifference.
▲ suasion: to predict consequences, to persuade.

LANGUAGE FORMS

On completion, students will have used the following structures:

▲ **Sentence types**

Conjunctive adverbs: "therefore," "however"

Adverbial clauses of concession: "unless," "although"

▲ **Verb tenses**

Caustic verb forms

Past conditional

Passive forms in the simple past and future tenses

LANGUAGE SKILLS

Listening: On completion, students will have:

▲ demonstrated understanding of the majority of face-to-face speech in standard dialect and at a normal spoken rate, with some repetition.
▲ demonstrated understanding of abstract topics in familiar contexts.
▲ demonstrated understanding of new vocabulary in context through guessing strategies.

Speaking: On completion, students will have:

▲ asked and answered questions fluently with minimal errors in the present, past, and future tenses.
▲ clarified meaning through strategies such as paraphrasing when misunderstanding occurs.
▲ adjusted the level of language used in face-to-face conversations in accordance with the formality required by the social situation.

Reading: On completion, students will have:

▲ interpreted both authentic and edited materials.
▲ identified main ideas and supporting details or examples from familiar material.
▲ guessed meaning from context by analyzing words, prefixes, and suffixes.
▲ made inferences.
▲ summarized reading passages.

Writing: On completion, students will have:

▲ expanded and combined simple sentences by adding modifying words, clauses, and phrases.
▲ written and punctuated complex sentences.
▲ written descriptive and narrative paragraphs, using correct punctuation.
▲ used transition words within and between paragraphs.

Some Common Uses of Capitalization

Topic: Uppercase letters

1. A capital letter is used for the first word of every sentence.

   Examples: The class starts at 9.
   Are they going to the store?

2. A capital letter is used for the proper names of people.

   Examples: Edith Piaf
   Albert Einstein

3. A capital letter is used for the proper names of places and geographic divisions.

   Examples: California
   France
   the Far East
   the Midwest

4. A capital letter is used for the names of nationalities, races, and languages.

   Examples: French   Asian
   American   English
   Caucasian   Russian

5. A capital letter is used for the days of the week, months of the year, holidays, and holy days.

   Examples: Monday   May
   Friday   Labor Day
   January   Christmas

6. A capital letter is used for salutations and complimentary closes.

   Examples: Dear Ms. Jones
   Dear Sir
   Sincerely
   Yours truly

7. A capital letter is used for the first word, last word, and every important word in the titles of publications, films, and other artistic works.

   Examples: *War and Peace*
   Of Mice and Men
   Cat on a Hot Tin Roof
   Beethoven's Symphony no. 5

 A capital letter is indicated by three lines under it. Find and mark the letters in the paragraph that should be capitalized.

nancy's birthday is march 20th. for her celebration, she is taking robin, alexandra, and michiko to see *sense and sensibility*, a movie based on jane austen's book. after the movie, they will all go to dinner at the brownstone inn.

Punctuation Marks

Topic: Recognizing and naming punctuation

Write the correct term under each punctuation mark. Check your answers with a partner.

Partner's name _____

Use these words.

apostrophe semicolon parentheses	colon comma	quotation marks question mark	period exclamation point

.

_____

?

_____

!

_____

,

_____

,

_____

" "

_____

:

_____

;

_____

( )

_____

Which three marks come at the end of a sentence?

1. _____

2. _____

3. _____

Which three marks can indicate a pause in a sentence?

4. _____

5. _____

6. _____

End Marks

Topics: Sentence conclusions, types of sentences

End marks are used to separate one sentence from another.

Use a period (.) :

- at the end of a sentence that states a fact (a **declarative** sentence).

> I am from China.
> Abraham Lincoln was the sixteenth president of the United States.

- at the end of a sentence that makes a request or gives a command (an **imperative** sentence).

> Please give me the key.
> Do not open that door.

Use a question mark (**?**) when the sentence asks a question (an **interrogative** sentence).

> What is your name?
> Where were you last night?

Use an exclamation point (**!**) when the sentence shows surprise (an **exclamatory** sentence) or delight.

> Look out!
> That was fantastic!

 Name the types of sentences.

1. Use only 93 octane gas.   _____

2. Did you enjoy the movie?   _____

3. I was late for class today.   _____

4. What a wonderful view!   _____

Using End Marks

Topics: Choosing end marks, creating sentences

Add the correct end mark for each sentence. Then check your answers with a partner.

Partner's name _____

1. Do you know where the book is
2. I live in Seattle
3. Put your pencils down
4. Be careful
5. Turn on the lights
6. Where did they go
7. That's wonderful
8. I should have asked her before she left
9. Are you still living in Los Angeles
10. I'm not going to take a vacation this year

Write two declarative sentences.

_____
_____
_____

Write two imperative sentences.

_____
_____
_____

Write two interrogative sentences.

_____
_____
_____

Write two exclamatory sentences.

_____
_____
_____

An Apostrophe Indicates the Possessive Case.

Topics: Common uses of commas, apostrophes, and quotation marks

Use a comma (,) :

- to separate two or more words or phrases of equal value.

> I bought milk, bread, apples, and soap.
> John likes to go skiing, listen to music, and play soccer.

- to separate a part of the sentence that is independent of the main thought.

> Yes, I will be at work tomorrow.
> She said, "I can't go tonight."

- to separate dates, numbers, and addresses.

> August 4, 1997
> 1,324,987
> 1414 Main Street, Los Angeles, California

Use an apostrophe (') :

- to indicate the possessive case of nouns, pronouns, and proper nouns.

> Do you like John's new car?
> Those are the teacher's keys.

- to indicate the omission of letters in contractions.

> This isn't the answer.
> They're going to go to the beach.

Use quotation marks (" ") to enclose direct quotations.

> He said, "I want to hire John."
> "I will not change my mind," she concluded.

Using Commas, Apostrophes, and Quotation Marks

Topic: Appropriate punctuation

Insert end marks and commas where they are needed. Check your answers with a partner.

Partner's name _____

1. I live at 72 West Carson Hollywood California

2. She is here every Monday Wednesday and Friday

3. He came in looked around bought some bread and left

4. The date is April 24 1997

5. Yes I will go to work

Insert end marks, commas, and quotation marks where they are needed. Check your answers with a partner.

Partner's name _____

6. He said I will never do that again

7. Help help she screamed

8. I was there he continued until 1993

Insert end marks, commas, and apostrophes where they are needed. Check your answers with a partner.

Partner's name _____

9. I can t she insisted

10. That s John s car

11. Where are you going and who s going with you

12. When we found a lost puppy we took it home

A Paragraph Usually Begins with a Topic Sentence.

Topics: Paragraph organization, clue words

A paragraph is a group of sentences that express or support one main idea. All the sentences in the paragraph *always* support that main idea. A paragraph usually begins with a topic sentence that expresses the main idea. Supporting sentences follow. They develop, illustrate, explain, describe, question, or argue the main idea stated in the topic sentence.

[Topic sentence]   [Supporting sentences]
I arrived in the United States in 1990. At first I lived in New York. Then, in 1993, I moved to Los Angeles.

[Topic sentence]   [Supporting sentences]
Paris is a beautiful city. Because of the beautiful lighting throughout the city, it is known as the "City of Lights." More than a million tourists visit the city every year to go to the museums, see the sights, and taste the food.

Paragraphs can be organized in several ways. Two common paragraph organizations are (1) chronological order and (2) by comparison and contrast.

1. Chronological order is often used for telling stories or describing an event. Some words and phrases used:

first	*then*	*at the same time*
second	*next*	*after that*
third, etc.	*finally*	

2. Organization by comparison and contrast is often used for describing a person, place, or idea. Some words and phrases used:

because	*for example*	*therefore*
the same as	*different from*	*besides*
too	*more . . . than*	*further, furthermore*
similar	*less . . . than*	*-er than*
like	*but*	*although*
however		

A Paragraph Usually Begins with a Topic Sentence. (continued)

Topics: Paragraph organization, clue words

Read each paragraph. First, decide which method of paragraph organization the paragraph illustrates. Then read the paragraph again and answer the questions. Check your answers with a partner.

Partner's name _____

1.   Some people enjoy winter, but others hate it. Inhabitants of Maine, for example, who are used to Maine's dry cold, are very uncomfortable in Florida's high temperatures and humidity. Similarly, a Florida native would probably suffer considerably in New England's winter sub-zero weather.

   a. Type of paragraph organization: _____

   b. What words tell you the type of organization? _____

   _____

2.   The process of making wine from grapes is a lengthy one. After the bunches of grapes are picked by hand, they are gathered in large vats and crushed. Next, the newly pressed grape juice is transferred to barrels, where other ingredients, such as sugar and other varieties of juice, are added. The juice ferments in the barrels, and its progress is checked regularly by the winemakers.

   a. Type of paragraph organization: _____

   b. What words tell you the type of organization? _____

   _____

Write a paragraph, using chronological order, to describe an event in your life.

   _____

   _____

   _____

   _____

   _____

   _____

   _____

   _____

Paragraph Writing

Topic: Writing supporting sentences

Write two or three supporting sentences for each topic sentence. Then compare your sentences with a partner's.

Partner's name _____

1. All sentences in a paragraph should express or support one main idea. (Use words such as *because, but, therefore, if . . . then.*)

   _____
   _____
   _____
   _____

2. I came to the United States in 1990. (Use words such as *first, then, after that, next, now.*)

   _____
   _____
   _____
   _____

3. T.J.'s is the best place to eat in Los Angeles. (Use words such as *because, for example, like, similar, -er than, too, different from, besides.*)

   _____
   _____
   _____
   _____

Now write your own topic sentence and two or three supporting sentences.

Topic sentence: _____

Supporting: _____
   _____
   _____
   _____
   _____

Practice 12

Paragraph Writing (continued)

Topics: Supporting sentences, comparison and contrast

Pick one of the topics. Write a paragraph comparing or contrasting

- two recent films.
- two television programs.
- two sports teams.

Topic: _____

_____

_____

_____

_____

_____

_____

_____

_____

Pick one of the topics. Write a paragraph describing

- a recent event in your life.
- a recent current event.
- a historical event.

Topic: _____

_____

_____

_____

_____

_____

_____

_____

_____

Dear Mother

Topics: Writing a general/personal letter, letter format

A general or personal letter is usually handwritten, but it can also be written on a typewriter, on a word processor, or on a computer. A general letter includes a number of parts.

- the date
- the sender's address (optional)
- the salutation
- the body of the letter

- a conclusion
- a sign-off or complimentary closing
- a handwritten signature

In a general letter, the positions of these elements are not fixed. The date, for example, can be positioned either at the top left or at the top right of the page, and some writers even place it under the signature at the bottom of the page. (The sender's address is usually not included in the letter, but if it is, it is located at the top right of the page, under the date.) The salutation always appears in the same place, however: on the left above the body of the letter. It is followed by a comma. In the body of the letter, paragraphs are usually indented (started farther in than the left margin), but this may also vary according to the preference of the writer. Some writers prefer not to indent the paragraphs and instead put extra space between their paragraphs.

After the writer has finished saying everything he or she wishes to include, he or she adds a complimentary closing or sign-off and a comma. The last line is his or her signature. Here is how a general or personal letter often looks.

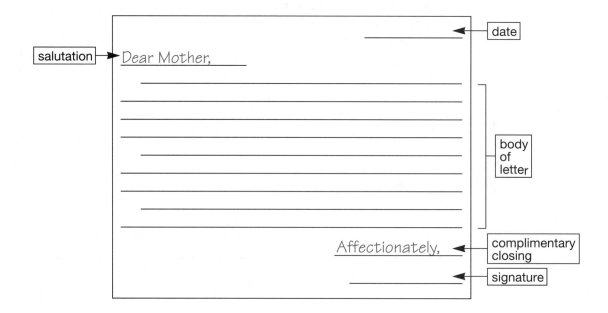

Practice
13

Writing a General/Personal Letter

Topic: Informal-letter writing

Using the personal letter format, write a short letter to a family member, to a friend, to a classmate, to a teacher, to a movie star, or to anyone of your choice. Before you start, make notes about what you want to include. After you have finished the letter, check your notes to be sure you haven't forgotten anything. Use any sign-off you wish. For example, if you are writing a family member, you will probably use "Love." Other possibilities are "See you soon," "Looking forward to seeing you," or anything else you think is appropriate for the person you are writing to.

Check your letter for errors in spelling and/or punctuation. Did you remember to include the date? Did you remember the commas after the salutation and the sign-off? Exchange letters with a partner. Can either of you suggest something that would improve the other's letter?

Partner's name _____

A Business Letter Is More Formal than a Personal Letter.

Topic: Using the business letter format

A business letter is more formal than a personal letter. The business letter format is used for all correspondence concerning business matters. For example, letters about personnel, orders, financial matters, inventory, and complaints are all business letters. A business letter follows a more rigid format than does a personal letter. Most business letters follow this format.

_____ | sender's information |
(name)

_____
(street address)

_____
(city, state, zip code)

_____
(phone or FAX #)

_____ | date |

_____ | receiver's information |
(receiver's name)

_____
(street address)

_____
(city, state, zip code)

Dear _____ :
(salutation or attention line: Dear Mr., Mrs., Miss, Ms., Attention, etc.)

_____ | body of letter |

_____

_____

_____

_____

_____

_____

_____ , | complimentary closing |
(Yours truly, Sincerely yours, etc.)

_____ | handwritten signature |

_____ | typewritten signature |

Writing a Business Letter

Topic: Using the business letter format

 You have seen an interesting position advertised in the classified section of the Los Angeles Journal. *The International Import Company is looking for someone who is able to read and write Japanese. You have worked in an office, your clerical skills are excellent, and you are fluent in Japanese. Write a short letter to Ms. Lori Ashland, the Director of Personnel at the company, 802 Western Avenue, Los Angeles, California 90483. You want to make an appointment to be interviewed for the job. Use your imagination and think of any skills or experience you could have that might make Ms. Ashland decide she should interview you. Mention them in the letter. Use your name, address, and today's date.*

Exchange letters with a partner. Check each other's letters for spelling and punctuation. Correct any errors that you find.

Partner's name _____

Name _____   Date _____

Following Directions and Test Taking

Topics: Understanding directions, following directions

Take this timed test. Wait until your teacher tells you to begin before you read the questions.

Time limit: 5 minutes.

1. First read all the instructions.

2. Write your name in the upper right-hand corner under the date.

3. Circle the word "name" in direction number 2.

4. Draw four small squares in the bottom left-hand corner.

5. Draw an "X" in each square.

6. Underline the word "instructions" in the first direction.

7. Draw a boat here.

8. Circle every number on this page.

9. Stand up and say your name three times.

10. Underline every "the" on this page.

11. Write the numbers 1–20 on the bottom of this page.

12. Ask the person on your right what his or her name is and write it here. _____

13. Reread direction number 1.

14. Now that you have finished reading carefully, follow directions 1 and 2 only.

15. Recheck your answers. Then put your pencil down.

Name _____   Date _____

Summary: Punctuating and Writing English Checklist

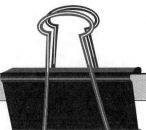

Check (✓) one.

Yes **No** **Need more practice**

☐ ☐ ☐ I know when and how to use end marks.
(example: p. 40. *"End marks are used to separate one sentence from another."*)

☐ ☐ ☐ I know when and how to use common punctuation.
(example: p. 42. *"A comma is used to separate two or more words or phrases of equal value."*)

☐ ☐ ☐ I can organize and write a paragraph.
(example: p. 45.)

☐ ☐ ☐ I can write a personal letter.
(example: p. 49.)

☐ ☐ ☐ I can write a short business letter.
(example: p. 51.)

☐ ☐ ☐ I can follow directions on a test.
(example: p. 52. *"Write your name in the upper right-hand corner under the date."*)

Write two other things you can say or do in English.

I can _____ .
I can _____ .

_____
Signature

Teacher's comments: _____

_____

Unit 4 Social Agencies and Contemporary Society

TOPICS

▲ Government officials
▲ Consumer protection
▲ Social problems
▲ Health facilities
▲ Immunizations
▲ Cross-cultural problems
▲ Common sayings
▲ Television

LANGUAGE FUNCTIONS

On completion, students will have used English for:

▲ factual information: to illustrate, to conclude.
▲ social and interpersonal relations: to express indifference, to express intention.
▲ suasion: to persuade.

LANGUAGE FORMS

On completion, students will have used the following structures:

▲ **Verb tenses**
Modals "should," "could," and "would"

LANGUAGE SKILLS

Listening: On completion, students will have:

▲ demonstrated understanding of the majority of face-to-face speech in standard dialect and at a normal spoken rate, with some repetition.
▲ demonstrated understanding of abstract topics in familiar contexts.
▲ demonstrated understanding of most of the language used in movies or broadcasts of a nontechnical or very general nature.
▲ demonstrated understanding of new vocabulary in context through guessing strategies.

Speaking: On completion, students will have:

▲ asked and answered questions fluently with minimal errors in the present, past, and future tenses.
▲ participated with increasing fluency in most face-to-face social conversations and telephone conversations, including those about work and current events, which contain complex structures.
▲ clarified meaning when misunderstanding occurs through strategies such as paraphrasing.
▲ adjusted the level of language used in face-to-face conversations in accordance with the formality required by the social situation.

Reading: On completion, students will have:

▲ interpreted both authentic and edited materials.
▲ identified main ideas and supporting details or examples from familiar material.
▲ guessed meaning from context by analyzing words.
▲ made inferences.
▲ summarized reading passages.

Writing: On completion, students will have:

▲ expanded and combined simple sentences by adding modifying words, clauses, and phrases.
▲ written and punctuated complex sentences.
▲ written descriptive and narrative paragraphs, using correct punctuation.
▲ completed forms or surveys.

Elected Government Officials

Topic: Federal, state, and local-level officials

With a partner, find and write the name of each government official. Look in the library or in an almanac, or ask someone.

Partner's name _____

Federal government

President   _____

Vice-President   _____

Your U.S. Senators   _____

_____

Your U.S. Representatives   _____

_____

_____

_____

State government

Governor   _____

Attorney General   _____

State Senators   _____

_____

City or township

Mayor   _____

City manager   _____

Consumer Protection Agencies

Topics: Agencies, the problems agencies handle

Many federal agencies have enforcement and/or complaint-handling duties for products and services used by the general public. Agencies also publish fact sheets, booklets, and other information to help consumers make purchase decisions and deal with consumer problems. If you need help in deciding where to go with your consumer problem, call the nearest Federal Information Center.

Some Consumer Protection Agencies

U.S. Consumer Product Safety Commission (CPSC)

Call the CPSC hotline between 10 A.M. and 3 P.M. weekdays to report a hazardous product or a product-related injury. Recorded messages on safety recommendations and product recalls are available at all times. Call or write:

> Product Safety Hotline
> U.S. Consumer Product Safety Commission
> Washington, D.C. 20207
> 1 (800) 638–CPSC (toll free)

Food and Drug Administration

Contact the FDA to report false product claims or consumer problems with food products, drugs, and medical devices. Call or write:

> Consumer Affairs and Information Staff
> Food and Drug Administration (HFE–88)
> 5600 Fishers Lanes, Room 16-63
> Rockville, MD 20857
> (301) 443–3170

Federal Trade Commission

Report fraudulent sales practices of products and services to the FTC in writing only to:

> Correspondence Branch
> Federal Trade Commission
> Washington, D.C. 20580

Office of Fair Housing and Equal Opportunity

Report rental or housing practice problems to this agency. Call the complaint hotline toll-free at:

> 1 (800) 669–9777

Better Business Bureau (BBB)

These non-profit organizations are sponsored by private local businesses. They offer a variety of services. These services include general information on products or services, reliability reports, background information on local businesses and organizations, and records of a company's complaint-handling performance. See telephone white pages for local listings.

CPSC is an acronym (shortened substitute word) made of the first letters of Consumer Produce Safety Commission. What is the acronym for the Federal Trade Commission?

What Agency Should They Contact?

Topic: Consumer protection agencies

Listen.

Situation 1

    I bought a new Cosmo computer for $3,200.00. When I got it home, I unpacked it and it didn't look like the picture on the box or the sample in the store. In fact, it didn't even say "Cosmo" on it anywhere. When I plugged it in, smoke poured out of the back.

    I took it back to the store and demanded my money back. The manager said that all sales were final and asked if I had ever heard of the phrase "Buyer beware." He said that I should have looked in the box before I left the store. Who should I contact?

Situation 2

    My two-year-old daughter got a small doll in her child's meal from a fast-food restaurant. The package said, "Safe for age three and under." I opened the plastic package and immediately cut my finger on a sharp edge of the doll. Then the doll's head popped off in my hand! This small piece could have easily been swallowed by my daughter.

    I went to the manager of the restaurant and showed him the doll. He offered me another one. I told him that I didn't want a new one, but wanted to warn him and his company about the danger of the doll to small children. The manager said that it wasn't his problem and that he just does what he's told by the corporate office.

    Then I called the corporate office and spoke with the Public Relations Office. They said the toy was safe. I don't think that this toy is safe. Who should I contact?

Listen again. Read the descriptions of consumer protection agencies on the previous page. Then decide which agency or agencies the person in each situation should contact and why. (You may use acronyms.) Check your answers with a partner.

Partner's name _____

Situation 1 _____

Situation 2 _____

Complaining Effectively

Topics: Consumer protection, making a complaint

When you have a consumer problem:

1. First contact the business that sold you the item or performed the service. Explain the problem calmly and accurately, and describe what you would like them to do about it.

2. If that does not resolve your problem, contact the company headquarters by phone or letter. Describe your problem, what you have done so far to try to resolve it, and what solutions you want. For example, do you want your money back, the product repaired, or the product exchanged?

   Keep notes of the name of the person you spoke with, the date, and what was done or said. Save copies of all letters to and from the company. Allow time for the person contacted to resolve your problem. Don't give up if you are not satisfied.

3. If your problem is still unresolved, contact the local, state, or federal office that provides help in cases like yours.

4. Taking legal action should be the last resort. If you decide to exercise this right, be aware that you might have to act within a certain time period. Check with your lawyer about any statutes that apply to your case.

Without looking in a dictionary or asking anyone, write what you think each of the words or phrases means. Use complete sentences.

1. "calmly and accurately" in #1

   _____

2. "resolve" in #2

   _____

3. "cases like yours" in #3

   _____

4. "statutes" in #4

   _____

Use the library or local telephone directory to find these agencies and organizations.

Federal Information Center: Phone _____

Local Food and Drug Administration: Phone _____

Address _____

Local office, Fair Housing and Equal Opportunity: Phone _____

Address _____

Local Better Business Bureau: Phone _____

Address _____

Make Your Letter Brief.

Topic: Planning a letter of complaint

Have you ever needed to complain about a product or a service? You are going to write a letter of complaint, perhaps to one of the consumer protection agencies in Scene 15. You may write about a problem you have had or about another consumer problem of your choice. First, read these **points to remember.** *After you have decided what to write about, use the space below to make notes about what you will say. Then write an original letter of your own on page 61.*

- In the letter, include your name, address, and home and/or work telephone numbers.
- Make your letter brief and to the point. In the first paragraph, describe the purchase. Include the date and place of purchase (or of the service), the name of the product, and the product's model or serial number.
- In the second paragraph, describe the problem, what went wrong, with whom you have tried to resolve the problem, and what has been done thus far.
- In the third paragraph, describe what you want done to correct the problem. List any documents enclosed (include copies, not originals, of documents).
- In the fourth paragraph, set a time limit for their response to the letter. State how you can be reached.
- Make the tone of your letter reasonable, not angry or threatening.

Notes

_____

_____

_____

_____

_____

_____

_____

_____

_____

Writing a Letter of Complaint

Topics: Consumer protection, writing a letter of complaint

*Write a letter of complaint, using the **points to remember** and your notes on page 60.*

_____
(Name)

_____
(Address)

_____
(City, state, zip)

_____
(Phone number)

_____
(Date)

_____
(Name of contact person)

_____
(Company name)

_____
(Street address)

_____
(City, state, zip)

Dear _____ :

(Paragraph 1) On _____ , I _____
                           (date)   (bought, leased, had repaired)

a _____ at _____ .
        (product or service)   (location)

(Paragraph 2) Unfortunately, your product (or service) has not performed
well (or the service was inadequate) because _____
                                                              (the problem)

_____ .

I am disappointed because _____
                                              (explain)

_____ .

(Paragraph 3) To resolve the problem, I would appreciate it if you would

_____
                        (the specific action you want)

_____ .

(Paragraph 4) I look forward to your reply and a resolution to my problem. I will
wait until _____ before seeking help from a consumer
                    (date)
protection agency or the Better Business Bureau. Please contact me at the
above address.

Sincerely,

_____
(your name)

I Lost My Job.

Topic: Social problems

Listen.

Situation 1

I lost my job eight months ago, and I haven't been able to find any steady work since then. Now, my wife, child, and I live in our car because we can't afford to pay rent anywhere. Most days I try to get some day labor to make enough money to buy food. We're good people; we've just had a lot of bad luck.

Situation 2

They were just kids growing up in the neighborhood. I don't know when they changed. First, they stopped going to school and started hanging out all day on the streets. Now, there are drive-by shootings in the neighborhood, and one 15-year-old girl was killed last week. There's graffiti everywhere. I don't feel safe walking down the street anymore.

Situation 3

He hit me again. This time he broke my arm. I can't live like this. He comes home drunk every night. I'm afraid he's going to hurt our two-year-old daughter. But what can I do? I don't have any money or a place to live. I told my mother about it, and she said I shouldn't get him mad and to just be a good wife. I don't know what to do, and I'm afraid of what might happen next time.

Listen to the situations again. Then write which social problems you think are involved in each situation.

Use some of these words.

drug abuse	homelessness	domestic violence	poverty
alcoholism	gang violence	unemployment	

Situation 1 _____

_____

Situation 2 _____

_____

Situation 3 _____

_____

Interviewing Classmates About Social Problems

Topic: Social problems

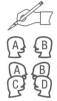

Interview three classmates. Ask which social problems they think are the most important. Are there any related problems? What do they think can be done to fix them? Share your findings with a small group or the class.

Interview 1

Problem: _____

Related problems: _____

_____

Can anything be done to help? Why/why not? _____

_____

What can be done: _____

_____

_____

Interview 2

Problem: _____

Related problems: _____

_____

Can anything be done to help? Why/why not? _____

_____

What can be done: _____

_____

_____

Interview 3

Problem: _____

Related problems: _____

_____

Can anything be done to help? Why/why not? _____

_____

What can be done: _____

_____

_____

Cross-Cultural
Discussion
2

Childhood Immunizations

Topics: Immunizations, childhood diseases

VACCINE	DATE GIVEN	DOCTOR OFFICE OR CLINIC

TB SKIN TESTS Pruebas de la Tuberculosis	Type*	Date given	Given by	Date read	Read by	mm indur	Impression
	☐ PPD-Mantoux ☐ Other ___	11/27/95	SB	11/29/95	SB	5	☐ Pos ☑ Neg
	☐ PPD-Mantoux ☐ Other ___	/ /		/ /			☐ Pos ☐ Neg
	☐ PPD-Mantoux ☐ Other ___	/ /		/ /			☐ Pos ☐ Neg

* If required for school entry, must be Mantoux unless exception granted by local health department.

CHEST X-RAY
(Necessary if skin test positive.)
Film date: ___/___/___ Impression: ☐ normal ☐ abnormal
Person is free of communicable tuberculosis: ☐ yes ☐ no
Signature/Agency: _____

PARENTS—PADRES
Your child must meet California's immunization requirements to be enrolled in school. Keep this Record as proof of immunization.
Su niño debe cumplir con los requisitos de vacunas del Estado de California para ser admitido a la escuela. Mantega este Comprobante; lo necesitará.

IMMUNIZATION RECORD
Comprobante de Inmunizacion

Name
nombre **Mallory Kerwin**

Birthdate
fecha de nacimiento **4/2/89**

Allergies
alergias

Vaccine Reactions
reacciones a la vacuna

RETAIN THIS DOCUMENT — CONSERVE ESTA DOCUMENTO

Name		Sex	Birthdate	
VACCINE vacuna	**DATE GIVEN** fecha de vacunación	**DOCTOR OFFICE OR CLINIC** médico a clínica	**DATE NEXT DOSE DUE** próxima vacuna	
POLIO 1	8/2/89	Family Medicine Center Anaheim, CA 92801		
2	12/14/89	Family Medicine Center Anaheim, CA 92801		
3	4/4/90	Family Medicine Center Anaheim, CA 92801		
4	9/17/91	Family Medicine Center Anaheim, CA 92801		
	11/27/95	Family Medicine Center Anaheim, CA 92801		
DTP Td DT Diphtheria Tetanus Pertussis (Whooping Cough) difteria tétano y tos ferina 1	8/2/89	☑ DTP ☐ Td ☐ DT	Family Medicine Center Anaheim, CA 92801	
2	12/14/89	☑ DTP ☐ Td ☐ DT	Family Medicine Center Anaheim, CA 92801	
3	4/4/90	☑ DTP ☐ Td ☐ DT	Family Medicine Center Anaheim, CA 92801	
4	9/17/91	☑ DTP ☐ Td ☐ DT	Family Medicine Center Anaheim, CA 92801	
5	4/27/95	☑ DTP ☐ Td ☐ DT	Family Medicine Center Anaheim, CA 92801	
		☐ DTP ☐ Td ☐ DT		
MMR Measles, Mumps, Rubella sarampión, paperas, sarampión aleman	4/17/91	Family Medicine Center Anaheim, CA 92801		
Hib Meningitis	6/2/93	Family Medicine Center Anaheim, CA 92801		

PM 298 (1/88)   BB 51187

Look at the immunization card and answer the questions. Then check your answers with a partner.

Partner's name _____

1. Whose immunization card is this?

   _____

2. Was this child vaccinated for polio? _____

3. Did this child have a TB test? If yes, when? _____

4. Was this child vaccinated for measles and mumps? If yes, when?

   _____

5. What childhood diseases are common in your home country?

   _____

6. Are children immunized in your home country?

   _____

7. Do you think it is important to have all children immunized against childhood diseases? Why/why not?

   _____

   _____

Cross-
Cultural

Discussion
3

Common Sayings

Read the sayings and write what you think they mean. Then write a similar saying from your home country. Compare your answers with a partner's or in a small group.

1. "Time is money." Meaning: _____
   _____

   Your homo country _____

2. "Actions speak louder than words." Meaning: _____
   _____

   Your home country _____

3. "Timing is everything." Meaning: _____
   _____

   Your home country _____

4. "All that glitters is not gold." Meaning: _____
   _____

   Your home country _____

5. "Don't count your chickens before they hatch." Meaning: ____
   _____

   Your home country _____

6. "Too many cooks spoil the broth." Meaning: _____
   _____

   Your home country _____

7. "Waste not, want not." Meaning: _____
   _____

   Your home country _____

8. "Don't look a gift horse in the mouth." Meaning: _____
   _____

   Your home country _____

Supplemental Activity 3

A Survey of Television-Watching Habits

Topics: Television, completing a survey

Complete the questionnaire. Go over and compare your responses in a small group. Then discuss these questions. Are TV-watching habits the same in your home country? What's different? Do Americans watch too much TV? Why/why not?

1. Do you watch TV?   Yes _____   No _____

2. How many TVs are there in your house?   _____

3. What do you watch on TV? (check one or more)

   _____ Entertainment

   _____ News

   _____ Sports

   _____ Shopping

   _____ Other (explain) _____

4. Do you watch TV programs in English or in your first language?

   _____

5. What programs do you watch? (list four programs)

   _____   _____

   _____   _____

6. Why do you watch TV? (check one or more)

   _____ To see a specific program I enjoy very much

   _____ Because it's a pleasant way to spend an evening

   _____ To see a specific program I've heard about

   _____ Because I feel like watching TV

   _____ Because I think I can learn something

   _____ Other (explain) _____

7. Do you have a VCR?   Yes _____   No _____

8. Do you watch prerecorded films (rentals)?   Yes _____   No _____

9. What kind of films do you rent or buy? (describe)

   _____

10. Do you record programs on your VCR to watch at a later time?

    Yes _____   No _____

11. When do you watch TV? (from . . . to)

    _____

12. How many hours a day do you watch TV? (total average)

    _____

Name _____   Date _____

Summary: Social Agencies and Contemporary Society Checklist

Check (✓) one.

Yes **No** **Need more practice**

☐ ☐ ☐ I can talk about consumer protection agencies.
(example: p. 57. *"Contact the FDA to report false product claims or consumer problems."*)

☐ ☐ ☐ I can locate local consumer protection agencies and organizations.
(example: p. 59)

☐ ☐ ☐ I can plan a letter of complaint.
(example: p. 60)

☐ ☐ ☐ I can write a letter of complaint, using a business letter format.
(example: p. 61. *"I am disappointed because . . . "*)

☐ ☐ ☐ I can talk about common social problems.
(example: p. 62. *"I don't feel safe walking down the street anymore."*)

☐ ☐ ☐ I can read and understand a child's immunization record.
(example: p. 64)

☐ ☐ ☐ I can complete a survey and discuss various TV-watching habits.
(example: p. 66)

Write two other things you can say or do in English.

I can _____ .
I can _____ .

_____
Signature

Teacher's comments: _____
_____

Unit 5 On the Job

LANGUAGE FUNCTIONS

On completion, students will have used English for:

- ▲ factual information: to illustrate.
- ▲ social and interpersonal relations: to approve/disapprove, to express indifference.
- ▲ suasion: to predict consequences, to persuade.

LANGUAGE FORMS

On completion, students will have used the following structures:

- ▲ **Sentence types**

  Conjunctive adverbs: "therefore," "however"

  Adverbial clauses of concession: "unless," "although"

- ▲ **Verb tenses**

  Caustic verb forms

  Passive

     Simple past

     Future

LANGUAGE SKILLS

Listening: On completion, students will have:

- ▲ demonstrated understanding of the majority of face-to-face speech in standard dialect and at a normal spoken rate, with some repetition.
- ▲ demonstrated understanding of abstract topics in familiar contexts.
- ▲ demonstrated understanding of new vocabulary in context through guessing strategies.

Speaking: On completion, students will have:

- ▲ asked and answered questions fluently with minimal errors in the present, past, and future tenses.
- ▲ participated with increasing fluency in most face-to-face social conversations and telephone conversations, including those about work and current events which contain complex structures.
- ▲ clarified meaning when misunderstanding occurs through strategies such as paraphrasing.
- ▲ adjusted the level of language used in face-to-face conversations in accordance with the formality required by the social situation.

Reading: On completion, students will have:

- ▲ interpreted both authentic and edited materials.
- ▲ identified main ideas and supporting details or examples from familiar material.
- ▲ made inferences.
- ▲ summarized reading passages.

Writing: On completion, students will have:

- ▲ expanded and combined simple sentences by adding modifying words, clauses, and phrases.
- ▲ written and punctuated complex sentences.

A Factory

Topic: Components of a factory

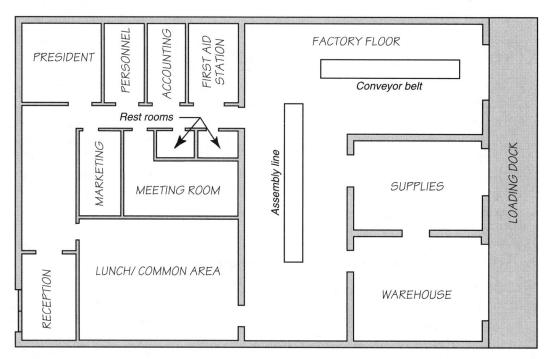

 Look at the picture of the factory. Write the names of the objects on the lines. Then write the room(s) where they might be located. Check your answers with a partner.

 Partner's name _____

Use these words.

forklift	vending machine	hand truck
time clock	trash bin	first aid kit

Found in

_____

_____

item: _____

Found in

_____

_____

item: _____

_____

_____

item: _____

_____

_____

item: _____

_____

_____

item: _____

_____

_____

item: _____

Your Work Area

Topics: Drawing a floorplan, describing a work area

Draw a floorplan of your present work area or somewhere you have worked. It can be an office, store, factory, or any other work area. Include and label all office and work furniture, equipment, machines, tools, etc. Take turns describing your work area to a partner.

Partner's name _____

Name _____   **Date** _____

Who Would You Hire?

Topic: Job qualifications

Listen.

Candidate 1   I just finished college with a degree in Comparative Literature. I'm ready to get out into the "real world."

Candidate 2   I've been selling copy machines for twenty years, and I'm ready for a change. I've been the number 1 salesman each of the last five years. I use a computer daily, but I would need to learn more about the products.

Candidate 3   My friends think I'm a computer nerd, but I just love computers. I have a Master's degree in Computer Science, and I built my own home computer system. I've never had a job before, but I think working in a computer and software store would be great!

Listen again. Decide which candidate you would hire as a salesperson in a computer software store. Explain why. Then discuss your choice and reasons with a small group.

_____

_____

_____

_____

A Job Application

Topic: Job applications

APPLICATION FOR EMPLOYMENT			
(Type or print in black ink only)			
Last name	First name	MI	Title of Position Applying for
Permanent Address Street _____ Apt. # _____ City _____			State _____ Zip Code _____
Mailing Address Street _____ Apt. # _____ City _____			State _____ Zip Code _____
Phone: Home or Message ( ) Work Phone ( )			Social Security Number

Work availability: Will you accept (Check boxes that apply)

Type of hire: ☐ Any   ☐ Full-time   ☐ Part-time

☐ Seasonal   ☐ Permanent   ☐ Temporary

Shift: ☐ Any   ☐ Day (8 A.M.–5 P.M.)   ☐ Swing (3 P.M.–11 P.M.)

☐ Nights (11 P.M.–7 A.M.)   ☐ Weekend   ☐ Rotating

Education: Highest grade completed _____

High School Attended _____ City _____

Degree or Certificate _____

College/University Trade/Technical	Course of Study	Dates	Degree, Diploma, Certificate
_____	_____	_____	_____
_____	_____	_____	_____
_____	_____	_____	_____

Professional License/ Certificate Possessed	Number	Date Issued	Expiration Date
_____	_____	_____	_____
_____	_____	_____	_____
_____	_____	_____	_____

List any other training completed which is applicable to job applied for.

_____

List any other job-related skills or equipment knowledge you may have which are applicable to job applied for.

_____

Practice 18

A Job Application (continued)

Topic: Job applications

Work Experience (Begin with your most recent experience. List all experience gained in the last several years, including periods of self-employment and military service. For full consideration, you must provide all information requested about your qualifications and work record.)		
Mo./Yr. to Mo./Yr.	Name and Address of Business	Dates From . . . to
Hours per Wk.	Name of Supervisor	
Salary/Mo. $		
Reason for Leaving _____ _____ _____	Duties _____ _____ _____	
Mo./Yr. to Mo./Yr.	Name and Address of Business	Dates From . . . to
Hours per Wk.	Name of Supervisor	
Salary/Mo. $		
Reason for Leaving _____ _____ _____	Duties _____ _____ _____	
Mo./Yr. to Mo./Yr.	Name and Address of Business	Dates From . . . to
Hours per Wk.	Name of Supervisor	
Salary/Mo. $		
Reason for Leaving _____ _____ _____	Duties _____ _____ _____	

A Job Application (conclusion)

Topic: Job applications

THIS INFORMATION WILL BE KEPT CONFIDENTIAL.

Ethnic origin (check one)

☐ **White** (includes Indo-European, Pakistani, East Indian)

☐ **Black** (includes African, Jamaican, West Indian)

☐ **Hispanic** (includes Mexican, Puerto Rican, Cuban, Spanish)

☐ **Asian or Pacific Islander** (includes Japanese, Korean)

☐ **American Indian or Alaskan Native**

☐ **Filipino** (includes Filipino only)

☐ **Other** _____

Sex: ☐ Male   ☐ Female

Do you have a handicap or disability? _____

Do you require special accommodation? _____

Are you a veteran? _____

Have you been convicted of a felony within the last seven years?

☐ Yes   ☐ No   If yes, explain _____

CERTIFICATE OF APPLICANT: I certify that all statements made in this application are true, and I agree and understand that misstatements or omissions of any material fact may be cause for disqualification or dismissal. I also grant permission for the employer to verify any and all information contained. Pursuant to the Immigration Reform and Control Act (IRCA) of 1986, all new hire applicants will be required to show proof of legal residence entitling them to work in the United States prior to becoming an employee.

May we contact your present employer? ☐ Yes   ☐ No

Signature _____   **Date** _____

- -

FOR OFFICE USE ONLY

☐ Accepted   ☐ Rejected   Explain _____

Action needed _____

By _____   Date _____

What's Taking So Long?

Topic: Communication between employer and employee

Listen.

1.	**Your boss:**	What do you mean, you want to leave early? You've left early every day this week!
2.	**Your boss:**	I told you I wanted this report finished 15 minutes ago. What's taking so long?
3.	**Your boss:**	Look at this! I can't believe that you painted it the wrong color.
4.	**Your boss:**	Why do you think you deserve a raise?
5.	**Your boss:**	We've got to get this project completed tonight. I need you to stay and work four hours overtime.

Listen again. Write how you would respond in each situation. Then work in a small group and discuss your responses.

Situation 1 _____

_____

_____

Situation 2 _____

_____

_____

Situation 3 _____

_____

_____

Situation 4 _____

_____

_____

Situation 5 _____

_____

_____

Asking for Permission to Leave Early

Topic: Employer-employee interaction

Work with a partner. Take turns being the employer and the employee.
Use your imagination and experience to act out each situation.

Partner's name _____

EMPLOYEE:

Situation 1
You've been late for work a lot lately. You want to leave work early
today because you want to go shopping.

Situation 2
You started work in the factory only last week. You want a raise, or
you're going to quit.

Situation 3
You've worked for the company for 20 years and have never missed
a day of work. You want next week off to go fishing.

Situation 4
You like to keep your work area neat and clean. The person who
works next to you is sloppy and never cleans his work area.
Complain to the boss.

EMPLOYER:

It's been a tough day, and you're two weeks behind on your
production schedule. You need every available worker to put
in overtime for the next two weeks.

*Reread each situation above. For Situation 1, think of another reason
you want to leave early. For Situation 2, think of another reason you
deserve a raise. For Situation 3, think of another reason you deserve a
week off or for requesting a week off. For Situation 4, think of another
reason you need to complain about the person next to you. Work with
a partner and take turns acting out each new situation.*

Partner's name _____

I'm Not Leaving Until I Get My Money Back!

Topic: Customer relations

 Listen.

Situation 1

Customer 1: Excuse me. Do you have this in a larger size?

You: Yes. I have more in the . . .

Customer 2: Hey! How about some help over here!

Situation 2

Customer: I want my money back.

You: Do you have the receipt?

Customer: No.

You: You have to have the receipt for a cash refund.

Customer: Well, I don't have it, and I'm not leaving until I get my money back!

Situation 3

You just saw a customer put a bottle of expensive perfume in her purse without paying for it. You are standing at the door as she is leaving.

Situation 4

A regular customer tells you that he finds one of your store advertisements offensive. He wants you to take it down, but you don't find it offensive.

Listen again. You are the only person in the store. Write what you would do or say in each situation. Then work in a small group and discuss your responses.

Situation 1 _____
_____
_____

Situation 2 _____
_____
_____

Situation 3 _____
_____
_____

Situation 4 _____
_____
_____

Name _____   Date _____

Role-Playing Customer Relations Conversations

Topics: Asking permission, making requests, responding

Ⓐ Ⓑ *Work with a partner. Take turns being the customer and the manager. Read the directions for each character and then role-play the situation.*

Partner's name _____

Customer 1

Your child's school is having a fund raiser for the school library. Each child is asked to sell 25 candy bars. Ask the store manager if you can sell the candy bars in front of his store.

Customer 2

You are a regular customer at the store. You need to buy some things, but you have to pay by check. Ask the manager if he will accept your check for payment.

Customer 3

You just slipped and fell on a polished floor in the store. You are not hurt, but you are angry! You want to know what the manager is going to do about it.

Customer 4

You want to purchase a sweater that is on sale. There is a small stain on the back of the sweater, and you want the manager to take another five dollars off the sales price.

Customer 5

You were in the store last night, and the salesclerk was very rude to you. He didn't speak English well and kept muttering in a foreign language. You want the manager to do something.

Manager

You own the small store and have to watch every penny. You accept cash only: no credit cards or checks. You know that good customer relations are important. Act out how you would deal with each customer.

TLC: Topics and Language Competencies 5, Unit 5   79

What Does the Employee Manual Say?

Topic: Understanding printed company policies

Listen to the questions.

1. How often do we get paid?
2. I don't understand. The pay period ends on the fifteenth, but when do we get our paychecks?
3. Payday is on Saturday. When do we get paid?
4. Hey, who's got the paychecks?
5. I lost my check and can't find it anywhere! What should I do?

Read the excerpt from an employee manual. Listen again. Answer each question according to the manual. Check your answers with a partner.

Partner's name _____

Payday

Pay periods run from the first through the fifteenth and from the sixteenth through the end of each month. Paydays are on the seventh and the twenty-second for the previous pay period. If a payday falls on a Saturday, paychecks will be distributed on the preceding Friday. If a payday falls on a Sunday, paychecks will be distributed on the following Monday.

Supervisors distribute checks to all employees within their departments.

Lost checks should be reported to the Accounting Office immediately.

---

1. _____
2. _____
3. _____
4. _____
5. _____

Lifeskills/Workskills

Multiplying Decimals

For Your Information

You multiply decimals the same way you multiply whole numbers. It is not necessary to line up the decimal points under each other before you multiply.

Examples.

A.

18.6 x .015 = ?

$$\begin{array}{r} 1\,8.6 \\ \times \quad 0.1\,5 \\ \hline 9\,3\,0 \\ 1\,8\,6 \\ \hline 2.7\,9\,0 \end{array}$$

◄——— multiplicand ———►
◄——— multiplier ———►
product ———►

B.

0.351 x 1.25 = ?

$$\begin{array}{r} 0.3\,5\,1 \\ \times \quad 1.2\,5 \\ \hline 1\,7\,5\,5 \\ 7\,0\,2 \\ 3\,5\,1 \\ \hline .4\,3\,8\,7\,5 \end{array}$$

After you find the product (answer), count all the places to the right of the decimal point in both the multiplicand and the multiplier.

In Example A, there are three: 18.6 and .1 5

1   +   2   = 3 decimal places

In Example B, there are five: 1.2 5 and 0.3 5 1

2   +   3   = 5 decimal places

Now, starting from the right of the product, count off the total number of decimal places in the multiplicand and the multiplier and place the decimal point in the product.

In Example A, the product is 2790. It has three decimal places; so the answer is 2.790.

In Example B, the product is 43875. It has five decimal places, so the answer is .43875.

Try these.

1. 2.2 x 1.1   2. 1.35 x 2.1   3. 0.4 x 2

Multiplying Decimals (continued)

Try answering these. If you have trouble answering the questions, work with a partner. Use the space below each problem to show your work.

Partner's name _____

1. 2.2 x 1.1

2. 1.35 x 2.1

3. 0.4 x 2

4. 3.45
   x 0.12

5. 0.003
   x 0.004

6. 4 3 5
   x 1.2

7. What is eight and seven tenths times five tenths?

8. Apples cost $.80 a pound. How much will 3.5 pounds cost?

9. What is zero point four, two, one times four point zero, zero, two?

10. If I walk 4.7 miles in one hour, how many miles will I walk in 2.5 hours?

Work Ethics

Ethics are principles of correct behavior or standards that govern conduct. Unethical work practice is behavior that does not agree with accepted conduct in the workplace. Decide whether each statement is an ethical or an unethical work practice. In a small group, discuss and compare your responses. Is each work ethic the same in your home country?

1. I always get to work late and leave a little early. I think it's OK because they don't pay me enough.

    ☐ ethical   ☐ unethical

    Why? _____

    _____

2. I work in a fast-food restaurant. We're supposed to pay for any food we eat, but I never do.

    ☐ ethical   ☐ unethical

    Why? _____

    _____

3. I am a sales representative for my company. The company pays me back for my travel expenses. I keep all my expense records and submit as accurate a bill as I possibly can.

    ☐ ethical   ☐ unethical

    Why? _____

    _____

4. I'm a security guard, and I work the graveyard shift. No one else is around, so I usually sleep for three or four hours.

    ☐ ethical   ☐ unethical

    Why? _____

    _____

5. I don't like my job. Whenever I want a day off, I just call in sick.

    ☐ ethical   ☐ unethical

    Why? _____

    _____

Supplemental Activity 4

Work Manuals

Work in a small group. Each person should bring in an employee policy manual, a work manual, or an instruction manual. Look over the manuals. Pick two for the entire group to review. Answer the questions.

Manual 1:

1. Type: _____

2. Table of contents? ☐ Yes   ☐ No

3. Illustrations? ☐ Yes   ☐ No

   Type (technical drawings, photographs, etc.)?

   _____

   _____

4. Language level (check one):

   ___ easy to follow and understand

   ___ can be followed and understood with some difficulty

   ___ difficult to follow and to understand

   Why? _____

   _____

   _____

Manual 2:

1. Type: _____

2. Table of contents? ☐ Yes   ☐ No

3. Illustrations? ☐ Yes   ☐ No

   Type (technical drawings, photographs, etc.)?

   _____

   _____

4. Language level (check one):

   ___ easy to follow and understand

   ___ can be followed and understood with some difficulty

   ___ difficult to follow and to understand

   Why? _____

   _____

   _____

Summary: On The Job Checklist

Check (✓) one.

**Yes   No   Need
                 more
                 practice**

☐ ☐ ☐ I can talk about different job applicants.
        (example: p. 72. *"I would hire . . . "*)

☐ ☐ ☐ I can fill out a job application.
        (example: pp. 73–75)

☐ ☐ ☐ I can explain and discuss different situations with an
        employer or boss.
        (example: p. 76. *"Why do you think you deserve a raise?"*)

☐ ☐ ☐ I can talk about various situations concerning customer
        relations.
        (example: p. 78)

☐ ☐ ☐ I can talk about, read, and understand a work manual.
        (example: p. 80. *"Supervisors distribute checks to all
        employees . . . "*)

☐ ☐ ☐ I can multiply decimals.
        (example: p. 81)

☐ ☐ ☐ I can talk about and discuss work ethics.
        (example: p. 83)

Write two other things you can say or do in English.

I can _____ .
I can _____ .

_____
Signature

Teacher's comments: _____
_____

Time Zones in the Continental United States

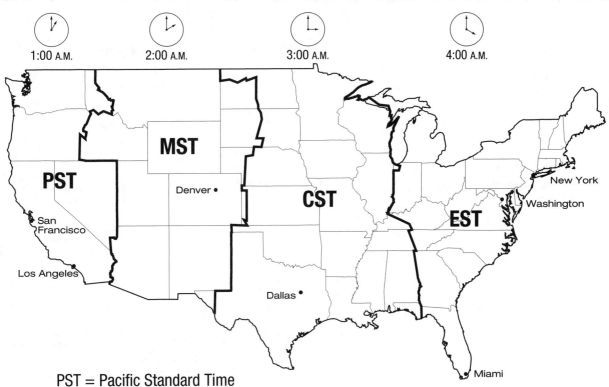

1:00 A.M.   2:00 A.M.   3:00 A.M.   4:00 A.M.

PST
MST
Denver •
CST
EST
San Francisco
Los Angeles
Dallas •
New York
Washington
Miami

PST = Pacific Standard Time
MST = Mountain Standard Time
CST = Central Standard Time
EST = Eastern Standard Time

U.S. Map

NEW HAMPSHIRE
Concord
MAINE
VERMONT
Montpelier
Augusta
MASSACHUSETTS
Albany
Boston
NEW YORK
RHODE ISLAND
CONNECTICUT
New York
PENNSYLVANIA
Harrisburg
NEW JERSEY
Philadelphia
Trenton
DELAWARE
Washington, D.C.
MARYLAND
WEST VIRGINIA
Richmond
Charleston
VIRGINIA
Raleigh
NORTH CAROLINA
SOUTH CAROLINA
Columbia

NESOTA
St. Paul
WISCONSIN
MICHIGAN
Lansing
Madison
Detroit
IOWA
Des Moines
Chicago
OHIO
Columbus
Springfield
Indianapolis
ILLINOIS
INDIANA
Jefferson City
Franklin
MISSOURI
KENTUCKY
TENNESSEE
ARKANSAS
Memphis
Little Rock
ALABAMA
Atlanta
Montgomery
GEORGIA
Jackson
LOUISIANA
llas
MISSISSIPPI
Baton Rouge
Tallahassee
New Orleans
FLORIDA
Miami

Hartford, CONNECTICUT
Dover, DELAWARE
Annapolis, MARYLAND
Providence, RHODE ISLAND

89

World Map

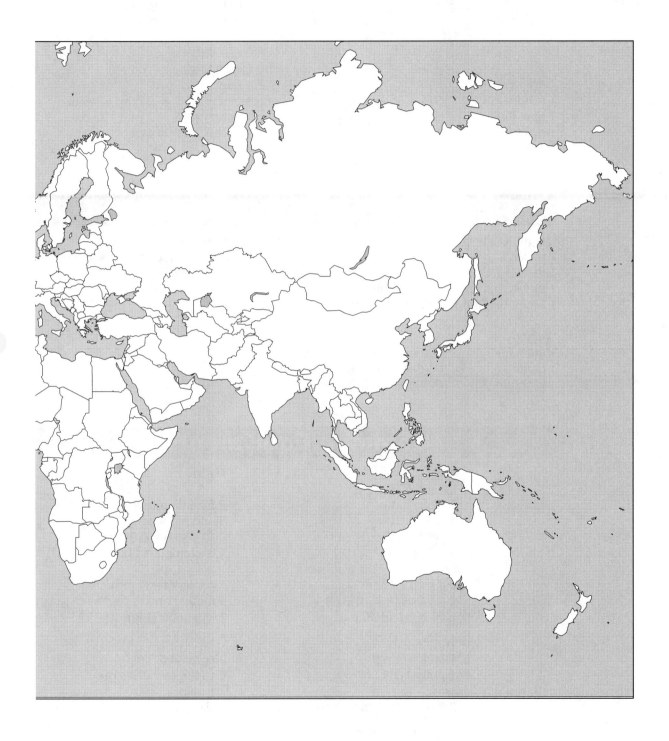

Standard U.S. Units of Measure

Length (Distance)
1 foot (ft) = 12 inches (in.)
1 yard (yd) = 3 ft = 36 in.
1 mile (mi) = 5280 ft = 1760 yd

Weight
1 pound (lb) = 16 ounces (oz)
1 ton (t)   = 2000 lb

Time
1 minute (min) = 60 seconds (sec)
1 hour (hr)   = 60 min
1 day (da)   = 24 hr
1 week (wk)   = 7 days
1 year (yr)   = 365 days = 12 months (mo) = 52 weeks

Liquid Measure (Volume)
1 cup   =   8 oz
1 pint   = 2 cup = 16 oz
1 quart (qt) = 2 pt = 32 oz
1 gallon (gal) = 4 qt

Common Metric Measurements

Length (Distance)
1 meter   = 1000 millimeters (mm)
1 meter   = 100 centimeters (cm)
1 meter   = 10 decimeters (dm)
1 kilometer (km) = 1000 meters (m)

Weight
1 gram (g)   = 1000 milligrams (mg)
1 gram   = 100 centigrams (cg)
1 kilogram (kg) = 1000 grams (g)

Liquid Measure (Volume)
1 liter (l) = 1000 milliliters (ml)
1 liter   = 100 centiliters (cl)
1 liter   = 10 deciliters (dl)

Common Equivalents

U.S.		Metric
Length (Distance)		
1 inch (1 in.)	=	2.5 centimeters (2.5 cm)
1 foot (1 ft)	=	30 centimeters (30 cm)
1 yard (1 yd)	=	0.91 meters (0.91 m)
1 mile (1 mi)	=	1.6 kilometers (1.6 km)
or		
0.4 inch (4/10 in.)	=	1 centimeter (1 cm)
1.1 yards (1 1/10 yd)	=	1 meter (1 m)
0.62 miles (6/10 mi)	=	1 kilometer (1 km)
Weight		
1 ounce (1 oz)	=	28 grams (28 g)
1 pound (1 lb)	=	0.4 kilogram (0.4 kg)
or		
2.2 pounds (2 2/10 lb)	=	1 kilogram (1 kg)
Liquid Measure (Volume)		
1 fluid ounce (1 fl oz)	=	29.5 milliliters (29.5 ml)
1 quart (1 qt)	=	0.9 liters (0.9 l)
or		
1.05 quarts (1 5/100 qt)	=	1 liter (1 l)

Temperature: Fahrenheit and Celsius

Fahrenheit		Celsius
212°F	=	100°C (boiling point)
100°F	=	38°C
32°F	=	0°C (freezing point)
0°F	=	−18°CT

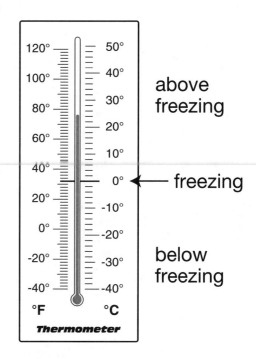

To change **Fahrenheit** to **Celsius**:

Example

1. Start with Fahrenheit degrees. 86° Fahrenheit
2. Subtract 32. 86 − 32 = 54
3. Multiply the answer by 5/9. 54 x 5/9 = 30°
       86° Fahrenheit = 30° Celsius

To change **Celsius** to**Fahrenheit**:

Example

1. Start with Celsius degrees. 10° Celsius
2. Divide Celsius by 5/9. 10 ÷ 5/9 = 18
3. Add 32 to the answer 18 + 32 = 50°
       10° Celsius = 50° Fahrenheit

> <u>A shortcut method to find approximate equivalencies</u>
>
> **To change Celsius to Fahrenheit,** double the
> Celsius number and add 30.
> **To change Fahrenheit to Celsius,** subtract 30
> from the Fahrenheit and divide by 2.

Irregular Verbs

be	was/were	been
begin	began	begun
bend	bent	bent
bite	bit	bitten
blow	blew	blown
break	broke	broken
bring	brought	brought
build	built	built
buy	bought	bought
catch	caught	caught
choose	chose	chosen
come	came	come
cost	cost	cost
cut	cut	cut
dig	dug	dug
do	did	done
draw	drew	drawn
drink	drank	drunk
drive	drove	driven
eat	ate	eaten
fall	fell	fallen
feed	fed	fed
feel	felt	felt
fight	fought	fought
find	found	found
fly	flew	flown
forget	forgot	forgotten
get	got	gotten
give	gave	given
go	went	gone
grow	grew	grown
hang	hung	hung
have	had	had
hear	heard	heard
hide	hid	hidden
hit	hit	hit
hold	held	held
hurt	hurt	hurt
keep	kept	kept
know	knew	known
leave	left	left

Irregular Verbs

lend	lent	lent
let	let	let
lose	lost	lost
make	made	made
mean	meant	meant
meet	met	met
pay	paid	paid
put	put	put
quit	quit	quit
read	read	read
ride	rode	ridden
ring	rang	rung
run	ran	run
say	said	said
see	saw	seen
seek	sought	sought
sell	sold	sold
send	sent	sent
set	set	set
shake	shook	shaken
show	showed	shown
shut	shut	shut
sing	sang	sung
sit	sat	sat
sleep	slept	slept
speak	spoke	spoken
spend	spent	spent
stand	stood	stood
sweep	swept	swept
swim	swam	swum
take	took	taken
teach	taught	taught
tear	tore	torn
tell	told	told
think	thought	thought
throw	threw	thrown
understand	understood	understood
wake	woke	woken
wear	wore	worn
win	won	won
write	wrote	written

Useful Words and Expressions

Certificate of Completion

has successfully completed

TLC: Topics and Language Competencies 5

Instructor

Date